Ex Libris

HER COURAGE RISES

50 Trailblazing Women of British Columbia & the Yukon

HALEY HEALEY

ILLUSTRATED BY **KIMIKO FRASER**

For anyone who has persevered through
adversity or persisted to reach their goals.

Heritage House Publishing Company Ltd.
heritagehouse.ca

Cataloguing information available from Library and Archives Canada
978-1-77203-425-7 (hardcover)
978-1-77203-426-4 (e-book)

Illustrated by Kimiko Fraser
Edited by Elysse Bell
Proofread by Nandini Thaker
Cover and interior book design by Setareh Ashrafologhalai

The interior of this book was produced on FSC®-certified, acid-free
paper, processed chlorine free, and printed with vegetable-based inks.

Heritage House gratefully acknowledges that the land on which we
live and work is within the traditional territories of the Lkwungen
(Esquimalt and Songhees), Malahat, Pacheedaht, Scia'new, T'Sou-ke,
and W̱SÁNEĆ (Pauquachin, Tsartlip, Tsawout, Tseycum) Peoples.

We acknowledge the financial support of the Government of Canada
through the Canada Book Fund (CBF) and the Canada Council for
the Arts, and the Province of British Columbia through the British
Columbia Arts Council and the Book Publishing Tax Credit.

26 25 24 23 22   1 2 3 4 5

Printed in China

CONTENTS

HELPERS AND HEALERS

POLITICIANS

ATHLETES

INTRODUCTION

W OMEN OF British Columbia and the Yukon have always been trailblazers. But they haven't always been included in history books and stories. The pages of this book are filled with women who lived fearlessly, unapologetically, and intentionally. With colour illustrations, these women's stories come to life.

These women were diverse. They were daring. And they blazed their own trails in life. Much like women today, they kept going when things got tough and adapted when things changed. They were aviators, gold rushers, authors, and bounty hunters. They lived life in their own way. Some fell under the spell of the Yukon, venturing north for gold (Lucille Hunter), to work in journalism (Alice Freeman), or to seek fortune and adventure (Nellie Cashman). Others were brave pioneers who farmed, hunted, fished, and supported their families during British Columbia's early days.

Some are well known, like painter Emily Carr and performer E. Pauline Johnson (Tekahionwake). Others are less well known, like professor Rosemary Brown and Haida artist Florence Edenshaw Davidson. Still others haven't yet received the credit they deserve, such as Frances Oldham Kelsey, scientist for the US Food and Drug Administration.

In some ways, their lives differed from those of women today: no internet, no social media, and very different rights and opportunities. But despite this, they share many similarities with women today. They celebrated life milestones like graduations, weddings, and having children. They accomplished great things and decided what directions they wanted their lives to go. They encountered setbacks, hardships, and difficulties. They faced adversity with courage, optimism, and a can-do attitude. They showed fierce determination in achieving their unique goals. In reading these women's stories, we can draw inspiration from them and even learn from the ways in which they reached their goals and coped with life's inevitable challenges. Their stories remind us that we can be our own kind of hero or heroine; that rather than letting adversity ruin us, we can use it to make ourselves stronger. And they remind us that we can leave the world a better place, making our own small difference where it matters.

This collection provides a fascinating glimpse into the lives of unsung heroines of the Yukon and British Columbia. The profiles are categorized by area of passion or expertise. It starts with writers, photographers and artists, entrepreneurs, miners, and adventurers, and continues with doctors and scientists, brave pioneers and homesteaders, helpers and healers, politicians, and athletes. I am grateful to have had the opportunity to weave this research into stories. My hope is that this book entertains, educates, and inspires others to let their courage rise.

Note of Truth and Reconciliation

This book was written on the traditional, ancestral, and unceded territory of the Snuneymuxw First Nation. Although some characters of this book were settlers and newcomers to the area we now call British Columbia and the Yukon, the author does not condone colonization or any of the shameful behaviours that accompanied it. The author fully and completely supports truth and reconciliation in all its forms and recognizes her own role in truth and reconciliation.

This book contains excerpts from *On Their Own Terms: True Stories of Trailblazing Women of Vancouver Island* and *Flourishing and Free: More Stories of Trailblazing Women of Vancouver Island*.

EDITH JOSIE

Newspaper Correspondent

1921–2010

Old Crow, Yukon

N O ROADS lead to Old Crow, Yukon. To get there, you must fly or arrive by riverboat. Located above the Arctic Circle, in Vuntut Gwitchin First Nation traditional territory, it was home to the remarkable Edith Josie. For forty years, Edith's newspaper column taught Canada about Old Crow—the people, the happenings, and Vuntut Gwitchin culture.

Eagle, Alaska, was Edith's birthplace and home until she was sixteen. In 1940, her family moved to Whitestone Village, then to Old Crow, which had only been a permanent settlement for twenty years. Before that, Vuntut Gwitchin people were nomadic, moving with the caribou. There, Edith trapped, tanned, and sold animal skins for income. Having only attended a few years of school, Edith learned to read and write from her brother.

In 1963, Edith became Old Crow's correspondent for the *Whitehorse Star*. She wrote her column, "Here Are the News," by hand at a wooden table in her log cabin, relating stories about hunting, trapping, berry picking, fishing, frigid winters, summers when the sun doesn't set, and people's everyday lives. Edith wrote about big changes: the switch from dogsled to snowmobile; the arrival of airplanes; the establishment of schools, health centres and churches; and access to television and the internet. Although she didn't shy away from difficult topics, her column focused on people's kindness and commitment to family and community.

Edith's column was reprinted in newspapers in Edmonton, Toronto, and across the world. Her distinctive writing style and gift for storytelling became well known and loved. She received letters from readers across the US, had a fan club in Vancouver, and even appeared in *Life* magazine. By 1964, her columns were published in a bestselling book that was translated into multiple languages and sold in Canada and overseas. Edith also raised three children, cared for her visually impaired mother, and studied at Yukon College. She even served as justice of the peace for Old Crow for seven years.

At seventy-two, Edith was still writing. She received numerous awards, including the Order of Canada and a National Aboriginal Achievement Award. In 2019, a statue of her was placed in Old Crow. Edith wrote with honesty and vulnerability and knew what all good writers know—that story is everything. For years, Edith brought her rich culture and news of her unique home to readers around the world.

E. PAULINE JOHNSON/ TEKAHIONWAKE

Poet and Performer

1861–1913

Vancouver, British Columbia

EMILY PAULINE JOHNSON was Canada's first famous poet and performer. She was born in 1861, in Six Nations of the Grand River, near Brantford, Ontario. Her mother was English and her father was a hereditary Mohawk Chief of one of six Nations that make up the Haudenosaunee Confederacy.

The youngest of four, Pauline grew up in a house called Chiefswood. She attended traditional school, learned cultural teachings from her father and grandfather, and was also well read in classic British literature, like Shakespeare. As soon as she could write, Pauline wrote poetry. Her first published poem appeared in *New York* magazine in 1884.

When Pauline was twenty-three, her father was killed protecting hardwood trees on Haudenosaunee reserve lands. Pauline needed money, so she decided to perform her poems. She hit the road and began a seventeen-year performance career. In 1893, she gave over 125 recitals in more than 50 towns.

In her buckskin dress and bear claw necklace, Pauline performed in a variety of settings from barns to saloons to private parties, and even the Steinway Hall in London, England. She performed for lords and ladies, and met Sir Wilfred Laurier and suffragist Nellie McClung. Pauline called herself Tekahionwake—meaning "double wampum," a belt of shell beads that records history and celebrates important events.

Pauline was unique and progressive. She read her own poetry rather than someone else's. She crossed the Rockies nine times and saw more of Canada than most, all while living in trains and hotels and supporting herself with her art. She wrote about Indigenous relations in Canada, challenged stereotypes, and demanded better rights and treatment for Indigenous Peoples in Canada. She published six poetry books and her work appeared in various magazines and journals in North America and Europe.

In 1909, Pauline moved to Vancouver, settling down for the first time. There, she reunited with Chief Joe Capilano, whom she had first met in England, where he was protesting fishing and hunting restrictions against West Coast First Nations. Her meetings with Capilano inspired her book *The Legends of Vancouver*.

When Pauline died, people lined the streets of Vancouver for the biggest funeral the city had ever seen. She is buried in Stanley Park, a place she loved deeply and which now holds a memorial to her. Her poems remain a strong reminder of Canada's first poet and performer.

MARGARET "MA" MURRAY

Newspaper Columnist and Publisher

1888–1982

Lillooet and Fort St. John, British Columbia

MARGARET MURRAY moved to Canada to marry a cowboy, but married a publisher instead. Margaret grew up in Kansas, to Irish immigrant parents. She was one of nine children and the family lived in such poverty that she chewed tobacco to feel less hungry. Margaret worked on her parents' farm, studied for a year, then worked at a saddle factory. Many saddles were destined for Alberta and Margaret began slipping notes into the invoices for the cowboys. She received several responses back, and decided to move to Alberta. On her way, she stopped in Vancouver and worked as a bookkeeper for a newspaper, the *Chinook*. She met a newspaper publisher named George, who halted her plans to move to Alberta and later married her. They eventually moved north to Lillooet.

In 1933, Margaret started the *Bridge River-Lillooet News*, making her the only female newspaper publisher in BC. Her newspaper guaranteed "a chuckle every week and a belly laugh once a month or your money back."

Margaret's editorials were feisty, spicy, and often controversial. Some stories she embellished; others were fully fictional. All ended with a signature phrase: "And that's fer damshur." Some people loved her editorials; others hated them. A woman once threatened her with a horse whip, and another time, someone broke into her office wanting to destroy an incriminating article.

Despite being a writer, spelling and grammar weren't Margaret's strong suits. What she lacked there, however, she made up for in business sense. Her financial acumen got her papers through some dire times, including paper rations during the Second World War.

Margaret always spoke up for what she believed in. And sometimes she acted on it, too. She was opposed to what she perceived as excessive waste from the building of the Alaska Highway. Once, she used a fishing rod to "catch" different unused clothing items from the job site, which she gave to less fortunate people in the community.

Margaret was outspoken, no-nonsense, and an individual. She was called "a whirlwind of a woman" and the "salty scourge of Lillooet" in *Maclean's* magazine. Margaret appeared in a documentary called *People of the Peace*, an elementary school in Fort St. John bears her name, and another newspaper she started, the *Alaska Highway News*, still exists today. Ma Murray is sure to be remembered as British Columbia's first female newspaper publisher.

ALICE FREEMAN
(FAITH FENTON)

Gold Rush Journalist and Teacher

1857–1936

Dawson City, Yukon

GOLD WAS what brought most people to the Yukon in 1898, but Alice Freeman ventured there to work as a newspaper correspondent for the Toronto *Globe*.

Alice hadn't always been a journalist. She was born in Bowmanville, in southern Ontario, and lived with a reverend and his wife because her family had too many children to feed. In Toronto, she studied to be a teacher and taught at various schools for nineteen years. Though teaching paid the bills, writing was Alice's true passion, which she pursued in the evenings and during summer breaks. Her real name was Alice Freeman, but when writing, she called herself Faith Fenton. Eventually she quit teaching altogether and, in 1894, became a full-time writer and editor. She was the first female magazine editor in Canada. A year later, she lost her job. It was then that Alice was asked to travel to the Yukon and cover the gold rush. She said yes.

To get there, she travelled with two nurses, the wife of a North-West Mounted Police officer, and 200 soldiers headed there to establish a Canadian military presence. They would take the all-Canadian Stikine Trail route. Even getting to the start of the trail was a journey: a few days in a railcar from Ottawa to Vancouver, five days on a ship called the *Islander* to Wrangell, Alaska, and four days by steamer up the Stikine River. Then, a three-month trek of over 200 kilometres began. There were fierce mosquitoes, bogs, gruelling blown-down trees, and knee-deep muskeg land. Alice woke at 2:00 AM and was on the trail before 5:00. After the trek, they paddled down the Teslin River to Fort Selkirk.

In September 1898, Alice arrived in Dawson City, Yukon. She was thirty-eight years old. She lived in a log cabin, where she wrote and coped with frozen ink and unreliable postal service to get her columns to the Toronto *Globe*. Once on the job, her days usually ended at 11:00 PM. Reporting had undergone recent changes, and it was popular for reporters to be involved in newsworthy events rather than simply writing about them.

Her articles told of happenings around Dawson, scenery, weather, news, and trail conditions. Alice fiercely defended the Klondike administration when she felt that other journalists criticized it unfairly. Once, eager to get an article out of Dawson in time for the bi-weekly mail delivery, she wrote a story about a hanging before it happened. The hanging didn't end up happening, so she sent someone to retrieve it. To Alice's relief, the runner returned a day and half later with the inaccurate story.

Alice had planned to leave that spring, but the spell of the Yukon had captured her. She decided to stay in Dawson, where she became the editor for the city's daily newspaper, the *Paystreak*. Alice had befriended the medical health officer for the Yukon, Dr. John Nelson Brown. Eventually, their friendship turned into romance and, in 1900, they got married. Alice continued writing and was the first writer to send a news article from Dawson by telegraph in 1901.

Alice lived in Dawson City until 1905, when she and John moved back to Toronto. She had seen Dawson City's female population grow from a mere forty women when she arrived to over a thousand when she left. Women contributed greatly to the community, and in 1904, there were even enough of them to form a women's hockey team!

Alice Freeman followed her passion and chased her dreams. Rather than gold, it was a desire for adventure and dedication to her work that drew her to the Yukon. Her writing delivered a taste of the adventure and excitement of Klondike gold rush to people in southern Canada.

ANGELA SIDNEY/
CH'ÓONEHTE' MA STÓOW

Writer and Cultural Historian

1902–1991

Carcross, Yukon

ANGELA SIDNEY was given two names at birth: one Tagish, Ch'óonehte' Ma, and one Tlingit, Stóow. She also had an English name: Angela. Angela was born in 1902 near Carcross, or Caribou Crossing, Yukon. Family stories were an essential part of her childhood. They told about the Tagish Clan System, the gold rush, and trade. The Tagish People had a large role in trade, being geographically situated between the Tlingit Peoples on the northwest Pacific coast and the Dene People of interior Yukon. Through stories, Angela learned she was second cousins with Skookum Jim and Kate Carmack (see page 59), who first discovered the gold that led to the Klondike Gold Rush. She spoke Tagish, Tlingit, and English fluently.

Angela wanted to ensure that Tagish stories and language were recorded for future generations, so she became a cultural teacher in schools and undertook her own research. She later noticed that Tagish stories were sometimes being mixed up with coastal Tlingit ones and, wanting to correct this, she took everything she knew and started writing.

She wrote several books, including *Tagish Tlaagú*, published in 1982, as well as *Haa Shagóon: Our Family History* and *My Stories Are My Wealth*, which detail everything from the Clan system to family trees, Tagish culture, tradition, and stories. Into her seventies, Angela was busy preserving her language, culture, and traditions.

Angela's love of stories also inspired the creation of the Yukon Storytelling Festival in 1988 after her niece found out that Angela had to travel all the way to Toronto to tell her stories to an audience. It grew to host storytellers from around the world. Angela was the first Yukon Indigenous woman to receive the Order of Canada. She believed in living well in both worlds—traditional and modern. She wanted her children to be successful in the modern world, but to always remember Tagish culture and traditions.

Angela spent thirty years preserving Tagish culture. She once said, "I've tried to live my life right, just like a story." On a plaque in Whitehorse is a more famous quote: "I have no money to leave for my grandchildren. My stories are my wealth."

CAPI BLANCHET

Writer and Seafarer
1891–1961
Saanich, British Columbia

THE SKIPPER sipped her coffee and wrote in a weathered notebook before her children awoke for another day of sailing the inside coast of Vancouver Island. The skipper was Muriel Wylie "Capi" Blanchet, a coastal explorer, writer, and mother of five. She refused to let difficult circumstances stop her from fully enjoying life.

Capi was born in Montreal in 1892, the second of three girls. She married and moved to Saanich, BC, where she and her husband bought a house and a boat called the *Caprice*. When she became a widow at thirty-four, Capi decided to rent the house out every summer and cruised the coast with her five kids and dog.

The Blanchets explored places that many people had never been: Kingcome and Seymour Inlets, Desolation Sound, Quadra and Cortes Islands, and the Skookumchuck Narrows rapids. Capi wrote about fishing in streams with unripe huckleberries resembling salmon eggs, tracking the weather by cloud and barometer, showering in waterfalls, washing dishes in the ocean, and cooking salmon on beach bonfires. They rarely knew what day of the week it was, and some nights they fell asleep under star-filled skies.

They saw Kwakwaka'wakw longhouses with intricate carvings of Raven holding up enormous beams. They saw shell midden beaches, Kwakwaka'wakw people fishing in cedar dugout canoes, and burial trees hung with coffins held up by cedar ropes. They explored backcountry trapper cabins and visited eccentric pioneers.

Challenges were plentiful. Capi navigated the *Caprice* through wind, waves, currents, fog, tides, rain, and ocean swell. She diagnosed engine issues and planned routes. She navigated through mazes of islands, occasionally enlisting help from her eldest daughter and son.

Capi loved writing and later wrote a book about her travels along the coast with her children. In 1961, the year she died, a Scottish publisher printed 700 copies of *The Curve of Time*. Later, two Canadian publishers picked it up, too. It was welcomed like waves to a beach, and continues to be popular today, especially among seafarers and coastal dwellers. In 1983, a book that Capi wrote for her children was published. *A Whale Named Henry* told of an orca trapped in an inlet near the Skookumchuck Narrows who befriended a seagull with a broken wing named Timothy.

Each year, more people read Capi's exciting accounts of boating along the BC coast. Her words and stories are likely to endure for many decades.

ELIZABETH QUOCKSISTER

Photographer and Cultural Teacher
1925–1981
Campbell River, British Columbia

ELIZABETH QUOCKSISTER was born in 1925 in in the Da'naxda'xw First Nation of Knight Inlet, on BC's central coast. Her mother was Katherine Henderson, a midwife from Alert Bay who lived to be 104; her father was George Glendale, a hereditary Chief.

As an adult, Elizabeth worked on fishing boats, at canneries, and as a nurse's aide at a hospital in Campbell River. This was all while raising ten children, caring for community members who were homeless or marginalized, and promoting her culture and language. She also found time for a hobby: photography. Having received a camera as a gift, she used it to take striking photos wherever she went. A collection of her photos from 1940 to 1960, displayed online by the Museum at Campbell River, do what excellent photos should: capture the moment, evoke a feeling, and tell a story.

Her photographs show remarkable range and variety: a woman in front of an intricately carved totem pole; a man in a sleek and shiny car. A child, bicycle at his side and cedar bark gathering basket on his back; two teenagers sitting in the grass, evidently in love. And all without any formal training.

Elizabeth was also deeply involved in preserving her language and culture, and spoke both Kwak'wala and English fluently. She learned traditional songs and dances and taught them to her children and others after anti-Potlatch laws were repealed. She also taught her children how to sew traditional regalia.

Food was a big part of Elizabeth's life. Her children remember her growing beets, potatoes, corn, and string beans. Her son George described the land as a "candy store," covered with berry bushes and apple and pear trees. Elizabeth smoked fish, canned various foods, and loved making desserts.

Elizabeth also helped others whenever she could. She saved many girls from the horrors of St. Michael's Residential School by finding them jobs as babysitters, which helped them escape and return to their families, community, and culture. In 2008, she was recognized by the City of Campbell River with an award for her public service and selfless contributions.

Elizabeth Quocksister's legacy of cultural teaching and photography is truly admirable. Her work chronicled changing times and adds to our understanding of history. And it can be argued that a better understanding of history can contribute to reconciliation—vital to a healthy, equitable society.

HANNAH MAYNARD

Police Photographer
1834–1918
Victoria, British Columbia

I T'S 1898 and you enter a building off Johnson Street in Victoria, BC. You walk through a shoe shop, up a staircase, and pull back a black velvet curtain. Welcome to Hannah Maynard's Photographic Gallery.

Hannah was born in Cornwall, UK, in 1834 and married her childhood sweetheart. They moved to Canada, first living in Bowmanville, Ontario, then in Victoria. Victoria was booming and Hannah wasted no time in opening her studio on Johnson Street. Photography was in high demand and Hannah had taught it to herself while in Bowmanville.

Innovation is evident in all of Hannah's work. Throughout her career, she experimented with cutting-edge photographic techniques, like image manipulation, mirrors, masking, and multiple exposure. Hannah loved self-portraits and composites that showed the same subject multiple times. One photo plays with trick photography and pokes fun at the ritual of teatime. It shows three Hannahs: one sitting at a table pouring tea and another looking at the camera from a picture on the wall, pouring milk on the head of a third Hannah.

Photography was an unusual profession for a woman in Hannah's day. Some people boycotted her gallery, not wanting to support a female business owner. But Hannah persevered, eventually teaching her trade to her husband Richard and even hiring an assistant.

In 1887, Hannah's career took an exciting turn. She became the first official photographer for the Victoria Police Department. Criminals of all sorts came to her studio for mug shots. Hannah cleverly used a mirror to get a full face and profile in the same shot. Hannah retired in 1912, not because she was tired, but because she wanted to give the next generation a chance. She died in 1918 and was buried in her family plot in Victoria's Ross Bay Cemetery.

Hannah Maynard was a stunning original—the late 1800s version of what we might call an "early adopter" of technology. It was remarkable enough to be a female entrepreneur in her time, but even more so to innovate the way she did. She constantly experimented with techniques decades ahead of her time. And yet, despite the complexity and unprecedented nature of her work, it has gone largely unrecognized. Hannah, a talented, creative photographer who made whimsical, haunting photos that are eye-catching to this day, is a surprisingly unknown figure today.

HAZEL ANNA WILSON/
JUT-KE-NAY

Textile Artist

1941–2016

Uttewas (Old Masset) and Vancouver,
British Columbia

HAZEL ANNA WILSON'S button blankets made a great impact on Haida art and Canadian culture. She's even been credited with the artistic rebirth of Haida culture. Hazel's blankets—made from wool, with images emblazoned and adorned with buttons, shells, and beads—tell important cultural stories and uniquely revitalized Haida culture.

Hazel was born in 1941 in Uttewas (Old Masset), a small village in northern Haida Gwaii. Her Haida name was Jut-ke-Nay and she was part of the Duu gwaa St'Langng 7laanaas, or Raven Clan. She survived St. Michael's Residential School in Alert Bay. While walking on a beach as a young girl, an Elder told her she was destined to make button blankets. Sure enough, when she was fourteen, Hazel started making them.

Hazel got married at eighteen, and eventually had ten children. In 1972, she left Haida Gwaii for Vancouver. She first lived in Port Moody, then Coquitlam, and finally East Vancouver, and continued to make and sell her blankets, earning enough to live and travel. She called it "travelling on blanket power."

Button blankets are a Northwest Coast Indigenous art form that started after European contact. Women adorned traded wool Hudson's Bay Company blankets with appliquéd designs and further decorated them with buttons made from dentalium and abalone shells, pearls, and copper.

Button blankets show identity: of a person, a Clan, or a family. They can be worn as ceremonial robes during ceremonies, feasts, and dances. Eventually, button blankets became an art form, with some being created as wall hangings. Some show lessons and teachings; one of Hazel's called K'aayst'gáay shows resilience in the face of uncertainty.

Though Hazel was a well-rounded artist who also wove Chilkat blankets, she was best known for her button blankets. In 2006, several were featured at the Vancouver Art Gallery. A series of seventeen called *The Story of K'iid K'iyaas* tells of Haida Gwaii's 300-year-old golden spruce tree, cut down by a logger in 1997. A 51-blanket series called *Two Perspectives* shows everything from the Haida welcoming European explorers to their population being decimated by smallpox, their culture and language being supressed, and ultimately their survival and hope.

Hazel's blankets remain in art galleries and museums in Vancouver and around the world—telling stories as beautiful works of Haida pride, art, and culture. Hazel once said, "Any kind of sorrow that would come into my life, I would turn around and just continue working on my blankets."

KATE ROCKWELL

Performer

1876–1957

Dawson City, Yukon

KATE ROCKWELL was a performer who autographed her photos with the phrase "Mush on and Smile." She was known for sporting pink tights, diamond rings, bracelets, and chiffon dresses.

Kate was born in Kansas in 1876, and was wild from a young age. She was expelled from several boarding schools and worked as a chorus girl in New York, Seattle, and then Victoria at the Savoy Theatre. Then she went to the gold rush. She worked in dance halls in Skagway, Alaska, then set off for Dawson City to be where the real action was. Kate climbed the famous Chilkoot Trail but got turned back at Lake Bennett because women weren't allowed in the wooden boats gold rushers took from there to Dawson City. She changed into some men's clothing and climbed aboard.

Once in Dawson City, Kate worked hard, performing six nights a week, along with rehearsing and memorizing scenes and duets. She also wrote her own skits and ballads, choreographed dances, and even designed and sewed her own costumes. Good deeds, like raising money for her friend's eye surgery and visiting prisoners in jail, earned Kate a nickname: "Sweetheart of the Sourdoughs." A "sourdough" is a person who has spent an entire winter in the north.

Performing during the gold rush was lucrative. On top of her base pay, Kate received a percentage from wine sales and tips—often in the form of gold dust or even gold nuggets. She also received hundreds of marriage proposals, but wasn't interested. That is, until she met a waiter at the Savoy Theatre named Alexander Pantages. She and Alex moved in together, and with her money, bought a theatre called the Orpheum. Together, they ran it, and Kate headlined, produced, directed, and worked as a hostess.

Eventually, the Dawson gold rush died down and moved to Nome, Alaska. Kate briefly moved to New York before returning to BC. In Victoria, Kate bought a nickelodeon, a small movie theatre that also showed silent films. She then went to work in Texas, performing in vaudeville houses during the oil boom. Alex married someone else that Kate had performed with in Texas. She sued him, settled out of court, and moved back to Dawson alone. Eventually, she ended up buying a homestead in Bend, Oregon, and remarried. Kate Rockwell was Dawson City's most famous performer, whose charisma and talent left a mark forever.

FLORENCE
EDENSHAW DAVIDSON

Weaver and Textile Artist
1896–1993
Masset, British Columbia

F LORENCE EDENSHAW DAVIDSON was born in Masset, on Haida Gwaii, an archipelago off the coast of northern British Columbia. She became a respected Elder and artist who made baskets and button blankets. Her work served as both artistry and income. She tirelessly worked to preserve Haida language and culture.

Florence was born in 1896 to high-ranking parents. Her father, artist Charles Edenshaw, was a Haida hereditary Chief; her mother, Isabella Edenshaw, was a basket weaving artist. At the time, Haida People lived in cedar plank houses along the beach, with totem poles above the storm high tide line. Florence slept in a cradle carved by her father and, as was the custom, had her ears pierced when she was a few days old.

Like many Haida families at that time, Florence's family lived in different locations depending on the time of year. They lived in Masset in late fall and winter, and moved for work later in the year. Her father carved and her mom worked at canneries and sold her woven baskets. Florence watched her father carve in his woodshed. He made totem poles, argillite carvings, rattles, bentwood boxes, Chief's staffs, and gold and silver jewellery. Florence learned to weave baskets and hats from her mother, who also wove place mats, baskets for carrying water, and baskets with covers. Her childhood was spent helping her mother gather and prepare traditional foods; helping her father with wood; playing on North Beach with cousins, friends, and siblings; and creating her own toys, like dolls and balls, made by stuffing moss into clean flour sacks and sewing them closed.

In 1911, Florence married Robert Davidson, and between 1912 and 1938, they had thirteen children together. All were delivered at home, some with no help. Along with raising the children, Florence harvested and prepared traditional food and worked at canneries in the summer. Some summers, she ran a small restaurant out of her home, where she sold freshly baked bread and pastries. Other summers, she sold pies and bread to fisherman. Her husband was a commercial fisherman, trapper, hand logger, carpenter, and in his later years, an artist. They also had a cabin and smokehouse at the mouth of the Yakoun River.

Florence endured many personal hardships. She lost four of her children when they were adults and her husband Robert died in 1969. She grieved for months and eventually decided to keep busy by opening her house to visiting doctors, dentists, researchers, teachers, and nurses. They signed her guest book and enjoyed what she called Haida-Canadian cooking. She also started making Haida-style button blankets. Haida People started making these blankets in the 1850s, when they were forced by missionaries to cut down their totem poles. Haida People decided to put their designs on blankets and adorn them with buttons.

Florence became a respected Elder known as "Naanii," the Haida word for "Grandmother." She appeared in two films by the National Film Board of Canada: *Haida People* and *This Was the Time*, and her life story was recorded in a book by Margaret Blackman, called *During My Time: Florence Edenshaw Davidson, A Haida Woman*. She shared her knowledge with others, acting as an informant on ethnobotany for Haida People in 1970, a linguistic informant for John Enrico, an Elder ambassador for museum openings, and a contributor to a multi-media curriculum.

In 1952, Florence's beloved home burnt down in a devastating house fire. With the help of donations from the community and a bank loan, she and her husband had it rebuilt. After this, Florence started making button blankets. She needed something to keep her busy while she coped. She bought buttons from Vancouver's Eaton's. Florence was the first person in years to make button blankets again. She kept it secret at first, because she thought people would laugh at her and call her old-fashioned. Her first button blanket took two years to make and featured a grizzly bear design.

In 1937, Florence travelled to the National Museum in Ottawa for the opening of the Northwest Coast Gallery. She gave Prime Minister Pierre Elliott Trudeau a button blanket she made. In 1939, she also painted a canoe that her husband and brother made to sell.

Florence lived through immense changes in her community. She revitalized Haida culture with her beautiful and unique button blankets, kept songs and dance alive during the Potlatch ban, and assisted in the documentation of Haida language.

SONIA CORNWALL

Painter and Rancher

1919–2006

Kamloops, British Columbia

SONIA CORNWALL is an inductee in the BC Cowboy Hall of Fame. She was also a well-known and respected painter and rancher who left a mark on BC's interior region. Soon after her birth in Kamloops in 1919, Sonia's family moved to the Onward Ranch, near 150 Mile House. Before she was old enough to go to school, Sonia could ride horses, swim, skate, and paint. After finishing her schooling, she roamed free on her horse, learning the local plants and animals. Without any formal training, Sonia became talented at watercolour, oils, pastels, and mixed media.

At twenty, Sonia lost her father. To help lessen the family's financial strain, she put her art on hold and worked full-time on the ranch. It was hard work and highly unusual for a woman at the time. Only in winter did she have time to paint.

In 1947, Sonia married rancher Hugh Cornwall and moved to a log cabin on Williams Lake without running water or electricity. By the 1950s, she had time to paint a few hours a day. Her bold yet simple paintings captured the landscape brilliantly. Active, dynamic landscapes showing pastures, fences, cattle, and poplars made people feel like they were there. Her fans said she brought joy to her canvas.

The famous painter A.Y. Jackson was a longtime family friend. He visited Sonia at her ranch, encouraging her and eventually becoming her mentor. Sonia taught herself techniques from library books and, inspired by Emily Carr, always carried a notebook.

Sonia was a founding member and later president of the Cariboo Art Society. She brought in artists from other places for new inspiration and techniques. She never wanted her paintings to look the same. After continual experimentation with techniques, she developed her own style of colourful and unromanticised depictions of the Cariboo-Chilcotin and its inhabitants. Eventually, her paintings were showed in malls, libraries, and galleries around BC, including the Museum of the Cariboo Chilcotin.

Sonia is remembered for her bold talent—always creating art from the heart—and her affection and respect for the Cariboo-Chilcotin. She made a name for herself alongside other Canadian artists like A.Y. Jackson, Tom Thomson, and Emily Carr—who all inspired her art. Sonia captured the Cariboo in all its glory: livestock, rodeos, barns, spring floods, snowdrifts, and of course, her other passion—ranch life.

EMILY CARR

Painter
1871–1945
Victoria, British Columbia

EMILY CARR is a household name on Canada's west coast. Vancouver's Emily Carr University of Art and Design bears her name. But her life story is less well known. Like a bold brushstroke on canvas, she painted over societal norms of her time and devoted her life to her craft.

Emily was born in Victoria in 1871, and from a very young age, she loved art, animals, and nature. At eighteen, she went to study art at the California School of Design in San Francisco. When she returned to Victoria, she taught art classes in her own studio. In 1898, she first painted the West Coast fishing village of Ucluelet, to which she would return over the years to paint totem poles. At twenty-eight, she went to England to study art, and on her return to Vancouver, she worked as a cartoonist, taught art, and painted in Stanley Park on weekends. She sold her art to make a living and to fund her travels to California, England, and France.

Emily faced some major setbacks throughout adulthood. The Royal BC Museum would not purchase any of the 200 paintings she painted over five years, even after they were shown at a large solo exhibition in Vancouver. They said her style was too modern and they weren't interested in showcasing Indigenous culture. Money was tight, but she was creative making ends meet. She turned her apartment into a boarding house, although the demotion (as she saw it) from artist to landlady was difficult. She even raised sheepdogs, rabbits, and chickens in her backyard. Anything to keep painting.

Eventually, her perseverance paid off. In 1927, the National Gallery of Canada, requested Emily's paintings for an art show in Ottawa that also featured work from Group of Seven artists. Emily eventually became affiliated with the group. For the first time she felt like she belonged. Her paintings were—finally—becoming recognized, a development that she valued more than the idea of her name being recognized.

Emily Carr left an enduring legacy. After her death, Victoria got a public art gallery—something she had wanted for years. Emily was a Canadian icon and the only woman to be directly associated with the prestigious Group of Seven. She lived life wildly and in solitude. And she loved trees, totem poles, shorelines, nature, and freedom—all poignantly depicted in her famous paintings.

JENNIE BUTCHART

Artist Gardener

1866–1950

Mill Bay, British Columbia

JENNIE BUTCHART created the world-famous Butchart Gardens. Born in Toronto in 1866, she grew up with her aunt and cousins after her parents died at a young age. Young Jennie was energetic, athletic, and loved trying new things. In 1885, she graduated from college with top marks and a true talent for painting. She married Robert Pim Butchart and they had two daughters.

In 1902, the Butcharts moved to Vancouver Island, where Robert later started a cement plant. At first, Jennie was painfully homesick, but she grew to love the West Coast. She worked as a chemist in the plant's laboratory. The first cement shipments went out in 1905. By 1909, the plant's quarry was barren: a gaping hole in the earth. Filled with rusty equipment, it was a massive eyesore below their house; Jennie was not happy. One day, she told Robert, "Let's plant it with flowers, Bob. Let's make it beautiful."

Jennie was determined to make her garden a reality. She called botanists, read books, and hired a Japanese landscape architect. She obtained seeds from friends or on her travels. The former pit became the Sunken Garden; it was covered entirely with plants. There was a Japanese garden, rose garden, Italian garden, and Mediterranean garden, with fountains, sculptures, and ornaments from their travels. By 1921, Jennie's gardens were complete. She named them "Benvenuto," meaning "welcome" in Italian.

Word spread and visitors began arriving. Everyone was welcomed, seven days a week, with no admission charge; Jennie wanted the flowers to be "free for all." She didn't mind if guests picked a flower and refused to post any KEEP OFF THE GRASS signs. She gave away garden fruit to local hospitals.

During the Second World War, Jennie barely managed to keep the gardens going with a skeleton staff. After the war, out of necessity, she and Robert began charging twenty-five cents per person for admission. Eventually, Jennie took a step back, but in 1939, gifted the garden to her grandson. She lived to the age of eighty-two.

Before her project, Jennie knew nothing about gardening, but by the end, she was judging horticultural competitions. What started as a way to cover an unsightly pit ended up as a garden with blossoms from far reaches of the earth—a charming place of great beauty and a top provincial tourist attraction that brings enjoyment to over a million visitors every year.

BELINDA MULROONEY

Miner and Entrepreneur

1872–1967

Dawson City, Yukon

BORN IN IRELAND, Belinda Mulrooney had many siblings. Her parents sent her to Pennsylvania, where she ditched school and started working from a young age. She owned an ice cream shop in San Francisco and a sandwich stand in Chicago, and eventually worked as a ship stewardess, where she earned cash bootlegging liquor.

From there, Belinda decided to join the gold rush. She was broke when she arrived in Dawson, but got to work setting up a store with supplies she had brought. Belinda thought to bring items others hadn't: silk underclothes, cotton cloth, and hot water bottles. She sold these for six times their price, and in under a month, earned enough gold dust to start a restaurant. After that, she bought some land, and had log cabins built; they sold quickly. Belinda was twenty-five. Some called her crazy when she decided to build a roadhouse at Grand Forks—where the Eldorado and Bonanza creeks met. She was right, though, and her Grand Forks Hotel did brilliantly. Belinda lived in a log cabin behind the hotel. She preferred her pet St. Bernard Nero's company to humans. Nero would pull her by sled to Dawson.

Next, Belinda founded the Yukon Telegraph and Telephone Syndicate, providing the poles herself. She partnered in a mine company and built Dawson's first high-class hotel. After this, Belinda founded the Yukon Hygeia Water Supply Company to bring Dawson City clean water. All this while tending to her many mining claims. At one point, Belinda's nickname was "Queen of the Klondike."

Life was not easy, though. Belinda faced legal battles over mining claims, including one against Nellie Cashman (see page 53). She got married in 1900, but it didn't last. The lawsuits eventually caught up to her. She sold the hotel, moving to Fairbanks at only thirty-two years old. She desperately tried to rebuild her fortune by starting the Dome City Bank in 1906, but it didn't work out. In 1908, she moved to Yakima, Washington, where she built a castle, ran an apple orchard, and invited her entire family—parents, siblings, nieces, and nephews—to live with her. Eventually, lawsuits forced Belinda to mortgage the castle and move to a modest house in Seattle.

Though Belinda didn't maintain her fortune, she lived a life of excitement and business highs. She is remembered as a figurehead of the Yukon and left an indelible mark on the Klondike as a brilliant businesswoman.

COUGAR ANNIE
(ADA ANNIE RAE-ARTHUR)

Homestead Entrepreneur
1888–1985
Boat Basin, British Columbia

"COUGAR ANNIE" lived the Vancouver Island dream—homesteading, being her own boss, and living life her own way—back when these things were a necessity, rather than a trendy lifestyle.

Ada Annie, or Annie, as she was known, was born in California in 1888 but moved to Vancouver in her late teens. She was working at her father's veterinary clinic when she met Willie Rae-Arthur. They married in 1909, and moved to a cabin and acreage on a remote West Coast peninsula.

Annie had many homesteading responsibilities—all while raising children and watching for lurking cougars. She devised inventive business ideas to solve financial challenges, running a post office and store, a mail-order nursery, and hunting cougars for bounty. In Vancouver, she'd brought in stray dogs through her back door, washed them, and sold them out her front door.

Shooting cougars was Annie's claim to fame. Some say she killed 65 while in Boat Basin; others, over 80. She was said to be a dead shot, earning her an epic reputation (and nickname) along Vancouver Island's west coast.

After Willie tragically drowned while collecting mail from the mail ship, Annie placed an ad for a husband in two farm newspapers. It read: "B.C. widow with nursery and orchard wishes partner. Widower preferred. Object matrimony." This was before the internet and online dating. Without having met in person, George Campbell was selected as her next spouse. He arrived in 1940, accompanied by a minister, who married them that day. George died four years later. Again, Cougar Annie placed an ad. Esau Arnold, a farmer from Saskatchewan, was chosen, and spent ten years in Boat Basin, until his death. George Lawson arrived in 1960, but left around 1967. Robert Culver, a poultry farmer from Salmon Arm, was the closest with whom Annie came to finding kindred companionship after Willie, but he later left to be with his children. Annie's garden prevailed throughout.

Annie was as hardy as her plants were prolific. At ninety-two, she still had wood heating and drank rainwater from her roof. Given the choice, she would have stayed in her garden forever. It still exists, and is mysterious and magical in a wild, secret way.

Cougar Annie had unwavering courage and overcame immense hardships. She carved out a life in a place where many people would struggle to simply survive. Although she is one of many determined pioneers, her story stands out.

SOPHIE MORIGEAU

Free Trader and Rancher
1836–1916
Kootenay Valley, British Columbia

SOPHIE MORIGEAU made quite the name for herself as a frontier businesswoman. Sophie was a free trader, meaning she led pack trains that brought supplies to different places. She's a legendary character to this day.

Sophie's mother was Métis and her father was a fur trader. She grew up in the Kootenays on Columbia Lake, lived on a farm in Montana, and attended St. Paul's Catholic Mission in Kettle Falls, Washington. She was married at sixteen years old, but ended it soon after, keeping the Morigeau name.

Sophie began running pack trains from Washington and Montana to bring supplies to miners. It was a professional vocation that involved transporting goods and raw materials by pack horses over great distances that couldn't be reached by railroad or wagon road. Leading pack trains was gruelling, hard work, but very profitable. Sophie was the boss of her own team.

Sophie was tough as nails. She lost an eye in a railroad accident, earning her the nickname "Sophie One-Eye." Legend has it she amputated her own rib after a horse-and-buggy accident and hung it on the wall of her cabin wrapped in a pink bow. Another legend said she was run out of Golden, BC, for bootlegging whisky from Calgary.

In 1872, Sophie bought over 300 acres of land on Lower Columbia Lake. This was a land pre-emption, meaning she had to work the land. She kept cattle and horses to do so. She continued free trading and used the property as her home base. In 1882, she opened a general store in Golden.

Eventually, Sophie retired from pack trading, deciding to give up the income rather than entrust someone else with her pack train as she had acquired economic stability.

Sophie did things that many women in her time wouldn't have dreamed of. She managed a ranch and worked a pack train—difficult, dangerous work in a time when it was very much a man's world. She's said to have walked in both European and Indigenous worlds as a Métis person. An elementary school in Fernie, BC, bears her name.

LUCILLE HUNTER

Miner and Prospector
1878–1972
Dawson City, Yukon

FEW WOMEN ventured to the Yukon gold rush of 1896, and even fewer were Black. Lucille Hunter was a Black woman who ventured to the gold rush by the toughest route—while pregnant. She became a successful miner and prospector, and the Yukon became her forever home.

Lucille was born in Michigan in 1878. In 1897, Lucille and her husband Charlie took a steamship to Wrangell, Alaska, then travelled the Stikine Trail—also called the "all-Canadian route"—to the Klondike, through northern BC. This route was chosen by many because it was (falsely) advertised by newspapers as the shortest and easiest route. Part of the appeal was that gold-seekers, or "stampeders," didn't have to pay American duty, unlike the Chilkoot Trail or White Pass routes. The brutal journey followed the Stikine River through thick bush, narrow trails, clouds of mosquitos, and thin ice. Many stampeders got gangrene or scurvy. Lucille and Charlie reached Teslin Lake and Lucille had a baby girl, who they named Teslin.

From Teslin Lake, the family of three continued by dogsled to Dawson and were among the earliest gold rushers to arrive, in 1898. They wasted no time staking a claim on the famous Bonanza Creek. Lucille did the hard physical labour of prospecting next to Charlie while also raising their daughter. They staked two other claims.

When Charlie died suddenly in 1939, Lucille continued working their gold claims in Dawson and silver claims near Mayo on her own. Each year, she trekked more than 200 kilometres between the two locations. After the gold rush, many gold rushers left the Yukon, but not Lucille. She stayed and continued mining and prospecting.

When Lucille was sixty-eight, she moved to Whitehorse, where she opened a laundry service. She maintained a fierce independence, despite going blind in her later years.

Lucille was the first woman and first Black person to be named an honorary member of the Yukon Order of Pioneers. She was a well-respected Whitehorse resident when she died in 1972, at the age of ninety-three. She persevered through much hardship and left a mark on the Yukon as a Black gold rusher, and as a female miner and prospector.

DELINA NOEL

Prospector, Hunter, and Trapper
1880–1960
Lillooet, British Columbia

IN A photograph from the Canadian Museum of History, Delina Noel wears a long dress and holds a grizzly bear she shot. She and her husband came across the bear, and Delina shot it once. She shot it again, and it reared up and started after them. They shot it again at the same time, and it went down.

Delina was born in Lillooet, BC, in 1880. Her family moved to Quebec, where Delina spent her childhood, and then returned to Lillooet when she was sixteen years old. Delina married a prospector in Kamloops and after the wedding, started working in a mine. She never worked underground, but held supervisory and business roles. In 1902, she became superintendent for a mill that processed gold ore. She also staked her own mining claims. Men at a mine she worked at once threatened to quit if a woman continued as their supervisor. Delina's husband supported her in maintaining her position, and in the end, nobody quit.

In addition to mining, Delina hunted and trapped. She continued doing all three activities on her own when her husband died in 1946. In 1958, Delina was awarded the Centennial Medal, which recognized her fifty-eight years of service to the mining industry in British Columbia. Delina's old cabin, complete with a fireplace made from local quartz, jade, and granite, lies empty on a mountain above Bralorne, BC. Delina has been hailed as BC's most industrious female prospector and mine developer.

ÉMILIE TREMBLAY

Miner, Store Owner, and Midwife
1872–1949
Dawson City, Yukon

ÉMILIE TREMBLAY spent her honeymoon climbing the Chilkoot Trail. She was the first non-Indigenous woman to climb it, and was an important figure in gold rush history. Though she never struck it rich, Émilie was a courageous woman who left her mark on the Yukon.

Émilie was born and raised in Quebec. She met her prospector husband while living in New York and though her family protested, she went north. The long journey included a rail trip across Canada and two ships through Alaska. From there, they took dogsleds to the Chilkoot Trail. After two months at Lake Bennett waiting for the snow to thaw, they portaged around the Whitehorse Rapids and poled a boat up Fortymile River. They arrived in Fortymile, Yukon, in 1894. Émilie's new home was a filthy cabin on Miller Creek with a dirt floor, sod roof, and glass bottles for windows.

At that time, Émilie spoke only French, but she taught herself English from a grammar book she packed. It was isolating, but Émilie persisted. She grew a garden on the cabin's roof and cooked for workers at her husband's mine. Many remember the Christmas feast she hosted, of roast caribou, stuffed rabbit, and sourdough bread, complete with birch bark invitations.

Though she loved the north, Émilie missed her family. She returned to Quebec to look after her sick mother, and it was then that gold was discovered. So although she arrived to the Yukon before the gold rush, Émilie didn't strike it rich with gold.

In 1913, Émilie and her husband moved to Dawson City, where they worked mining claims. She befriended priests and raised money for charities. Though she never had children of her own, Émilie was a midwife and godmother to many children. She cared for sick miners and adopted her six-year-old niece. She also opened and ran a dry goods store for thirty years. When her husband died, she remarried and moved to a cabin where the Bonanza and Eldorado Creeks meet. At seventy-five, she moved to Victoria, where she spent the rest of her life.

Émilie was involved in her community, was friends with Nellie Cashman (see page 53), and knew Martha Black (see page 113). She opened her house to travellers, orphans, widows, and missionaries. She knit hundreds of pairs of socks for soldiers during the First World War. A French school in Whitehorse is named after her. She is remembered as a brave and courageous pioneer.

NELLIE CASHMAN

Miner, Musher, and Businesswoman
1845–1925
Dawson City, Yukon

NEWSPAPERS CLAIMED that the Yukon gold rush was no place for a woman. Nellie Cashman proved them wrong. Though she was one of many stampeders, she was unique—a woman who did her own mining, and made money doing it. Unlike many gold rushers, Nellie had experience. She also always had another business as back up. Some of the people who made the most money in the Klondike were the ones who "mined the miners" with essential businesses and in-demand services, including Nellie.

Nellie was born in Ireland and moved to Boston with her mom and sister. She worked all over the United States until someone advised her to go to Canada's west. She mined in Nevada and Arizona, eventually heading to the Klondike. In 1875, she took the gruelling Stikine Trail to the Yukon, wearing men's clothes, a long coat, and rubber boots.

Though she was fifty years old, much older than many of the miners, that didn't slow her down. She set to work purchasing mining claims. She worked them mostly herself, accessing them by snowshoe or dogsled. When one near Bonanza Creek made her much gold, she put it toward more claims. Nellie couldn't file new claims herself because she was an unmarried woman; she had to hire or partner with men, or purchase claims that were already filed. Several times, Nellie was accused of encroaching on other peoples' claims (including Belinda Mulrooney's—see page 41). She appealed the rulings and was found in good faith. Health issues also slowed her down a few times, and she had intestinal surgery. Nellie was extremely generous with her mining riches. She donated much of the money or used it to care for her nieces and nephews as well as the sick and injured.

Nellie often travelled long distances by dogsled to check her mines. Once, she embarked on a 17-day, over-1200-kilometre long dogsled trip from Nolan Creek to Nenana, Alaska. This trip would compare with the modern-day epic dogsled race called the Iditarod—done by ultra-fit, tough mushers with modern equipment. Nellie did it in 1923 at seventy-eight years old!

Nellie Cashman loved the north—its remoteness, the frozen landscapes, and hearing sled dogs howl. She was respected and loved by all. She even had her face on an American "Legends of the West" postage stamp. To this day, she is remembered as one of the Klondike's top miners, mushers, and businesswomen.

LILIAN BLAND

Aviator and Homesteader
1878–1971
Quatsino Sound, British Columbia

LILIAN BLAND was the first woman in the world to design, build, and fly her own plane. Her flying fixation came about from watching gulls soar and seeing a postcard of Louis Blériot's 1909 flight over the English Channel. Lilian desperately wanted to fly, but couldn't find anyone to teach her, so she took matters into her own hands. She built a glider and hired the garden boy to be her mechanic. She bought a twenty-horsepower engine and didn't give up, even after the props flew off in splinters during testing. She named her plane the *Mayfly*. Its first flight was in a bull pasture, complete with an aggravated bull to add to the adventure.

Lilian Bland was born in England, in 1878. Her mother died when she was young, and her artist father took her with him on his world travels. Lilian worked as a journalist from 1903 to 1908, writing instructional articles about car racing, hunting, and horse jumping.

A year after she got married, Lilian and her husband Charles Bland moved to Quatsino Sound on northern Vancouver Island, where they built a homestead. Homesteading life was arduous. Clearing stumps for gardens was back-breaking work, and there was endless wood to chop. No roads connected to the outside world; getting anywhere involved boating. Their marriage was turbulent. Wolves howled outside their cabin. Money was tight.

In 1913, Lilian had a baby girl named Patricia. When Patricia was older, she and Lilian planned to start a fur farm together. They secured a licence and registered a trapline, but would never use either. When Patricia was sixteen, she contracted a tetanus infection that ultimately killed her. Lilian was devastated and eventually returned to England alone. She found happiness there, where she wore trousers, painted, gambled, gardened, and played the stock market. She didn't like talking about her time in Canada. The grief was a continual challenge, but finances were no problem. She fared well in her stock market ventures and retired to a cliffside estate overlooking the sea in Cornwall. She was a spry older woman and lived alone by choice.

Lilian was talented in many areas: equestrianism, journalism, painting, gardening, photography, shooting, driving, and flying. She searched for truth and freedom, and found them—along with heartbreak—in the wilds of northern Vancouver Island.

DOROTHY BLACKMORE

Ship Captain
1914–1996
Port Alberni, British Columbia

D OROTHY BLACKMORE rescued two loggers stranded for two days on a timber-cruising and oyster-harvesting trip gone wrong. She expertly navigated her boat through gale-force winds and fierce waves before reaching the point of land where the two men awaited rescue.

Dorothy Blackmore was born and raised in Port Alberni, BC. Her father, George Blackmore, owned Blackmore Marine Services, primarily a water taxi service. Her older brother had no interest in boats, so George taught Dorothy the family business. At ten years old, she was driving solo. After high school, she drove full-time. Speed was essential—the first boat there got the job. She qualified for her master ship captain papers at twenty-one years old, but could not get certified. In 1935, many industries still did not consider women to be "persons," no matter what the law said. Federal laws finally changed, allowing women to earn their papers. Twenty-three-year-old Dorothy, the first female sea captain in Canada, made history. She was featured in headlines like "Coast Girl Picks Life on Tugboat" and "Madame Captain." Photos show Dorothy in marine coveralls at the helm, smiling as big as a lottery winner, speeding through the water.

Dorothy was a master ship captain from 1924 to 1957, often driving over the volatile, unpredictable waters of the "graveyard of the Pacific." She tax-ied loggers from Port Alberni to logging camps, took personnel to air force stations during the Second World War, and helped incoming freighters with docking lines. She was a member of the Merchant Marine (highly unusual for a woman at that time), and later also became a third class engineer. Much work was done in the *Commodore III*—a 28-foot, 30-knot, twin-engine speedboat. When her father fell ill, Dorothy took over Blackmore Marine Services. After the war, she married a Royal Canadian Air Force squadron leader named Pitt Clayton, and together, they ran sport fishing boats for a company they named Port Boat House, which still exists today.

Dorothy loved work. She didn't mind being on call twenty-four hours a day and heading out by boat when a freighter arrived during off-hours. An article in *Pacific Motor Boat* magazine in 1945 quotes her as saying she would "go crazy if she had to teach or work in a bank, like her sisters." Dorothy was casual about her accomplishments, apparently never thinking what she did was extraordinary. To her, driving fast boats was just another day at work.

KATE CARMACK/
SHAAW TLÁA

Discoverer of Gold

1857–1920

Carcross, Yukon

I N THE SUMMER of 1896, Kate Carmack was camped at the tributary of the Klondike and Yukon Rivers with her husband, brother, and nephew. One of them found a gold nugget in one of the creeks that would spur the world's largest gold rush. Kate's husband George registered two claims (one for each of them), while her brother and nephew registered a claim each for themselves. Afterwards, George boasted of the discovery in Fortymile. Word spread quickly to Seattle, San Francisco, Vancouver, and Edmonton, and soon, people from across the world and from all walks of life flocked to the Yukon, fuelled by gold lust.

Much debate has been had over who picked the nugget from the creek that summer day. George claimed it was him, while many accounts credit Kate's brother Skookum Jim. Other accounts claim Kate herself found the nugget while collecting drinking water. Some stories don't even credit Kate as being present during the discovery. Kate's life was not easy, but she was an important part of the Yukon's history.

Kate Carmack was born near Lake Bennett, Yukon, around 1857. She was one of eight children born to her Tagish mother and Tlingit father. She lived a traditional life as a nomadic hunter-gatherer, spending spring and summer fishing on rivers, and fall and winter in the forests hunting moose and caribou. After Kate's first husband and daughter died of influenza, she married George Carmack, a non-Indigenous man who had been married to one of Kate's sisters (who had also died of influenza). George learned the language and the two lived in Dyea, near Skagway, and then near Lake Tagish. They lived a traditional Tagish lifestyle, fishing, hunting, and trapping. Kate was a good hunter and tanned and sewed hides for moccasins, mukluks, and mittens. They opened a trading post near Five Finger Rapids that Kate operated while pregnant and while George was away building a church in Fort Selkirk. Their daughter was born in 1893, and they named her Graphie Grace. Later, they moved near the Klondike River to fish and so Kate could be near family. That's when the famous gold nugget was discovered that would start the world's greatest gold rush.

After the discovery, Kate, George, and Graphie used some of their newfound wealth to travel to California and visit George's family. A portrait, likely taken in Seattle, shows Kate with her hair in a bun sporting her famous solid gold nugget necklace.

Jennifer Duncan's book, *Frontier Spirit: The Brave Women of the Klondike,* discusses how Kate's life took a sad turn in 1900, when George left Kate and Graphie in Seattle after some conflicts over Kate's apparent drinking. George ended his business partnerships with Kate, her brother, and nephew, and married another woman a few months later. Kate tried to divorce George and charge him with adultery, but their marriage wasn't seen as legal in the eyes of the law because it was a Tagish wedding. She returned to her Yukon village, only to find it had been removed to make room for the White Pass and Yukon Railway. Her brother Skookum Jim (also known as Keish) built her a cabin in Caribou Crossing (now called Carcross), and she did beadwork and photography for tourists there.

Kate's life shows a darker side of the gold rush: one where traditional lands were invaded, sustainable lifestyles interrupted, and people, whose rightful homes were lost, were also affected by disease, alcohol, and greed. Kate endured deep sorrow brought on by massive changes to her land, but held on to her traditional way of life. She died in 1920 and is featured on a mural on the Yukon's Chamber of Mines building in Whitehorse. She was finally credited as a discoverer of gold and, in October 2018, was inducted into the Canadian Mining Hall of Fame. Whether it was Kate's discovery or she was merely present for it, that gold nugget changed the Yukon and Kate's life forever.

MINNIE PATERSON

Shipwreck Heroine
1878–1911
Bamfield, British Columbia

MINNIE PATERSON embarked on an epic night mission to save some shipwrecked sailors on the coast near her lighthouse home. Earlier that evening, Minnie's husband, the lightkeeper at the Cape Beale lighthouse, noticed a ship at sea in obvious distress. Through a telescope, Minnie saw men clinging to the ship's rigging while it got pummelled by waves. Normally, Tom and Minnie would help ships by telegraphing to Bamfield, a small village that lay eight kilometres away. Tonight, though, the telegraph line was broken from the storm; the only hope of saving the men was getting word to the *Quadra*, a government steamer that normally carried out mail, supply, and fuel deliveries as well as law enforcement. The ship, under the command of Captain Charles Hackett, was docked off Bamfield Inlet. Tom couldn't leave the lighthouse, so Minnie volunteered. She called their collie Yarrow, grabbed a lantern, and stepped out the door. She closed the door behind her.

She half ran, half walked through gale-force winds and thick rainforest. The trail was not well marked—and not much of a trail most of the time. Hours later and after much hard exertion in the cold and wet, Minnie finally arrived at Bamfield Inlet. But the rowboat that was needed to row to the *Quadra* was not there; her journey was not over yet. She continued on and at last dragged herself up the steps to the linesman's house. Annie McKay, the linesman's wife and a friend of Minnie's, answered the door. Shocked, she told Minnie that her husband was out fixing the telegraph line. Minnie relayed the situation to Annie, and together, they got in a small skiff and rowed through the angry sea toward the *Quadra*, taking turns bailing rain out of the boat. They arrived at the ship and quickly informed the captain about the shipwreck off Cape Beale, and he set off immediately at full steam toward it. Minnie's message was delivered; her mission was complete.

Back at her cabin, Annie readied a bed and tea, assuming Minnie would stay the night and rest. Minnie accepted some tea but refused the bed, saying, "Thank you, Annie, but my baby needs me." Her youngest child was still nursing, so she left and began hiking back the way she came. She was hypothermically cold and wet, but made it back home to nurse her baby. A week later, Minnie discovered her harrowing journey had been worth it: all ten sailors on board had been rescued. Minnie was a heroine.

Minnie was born in Penetanguishene, Ontario, and she grew up in the Alberni Valley, a region between modern-day Parksville and Sproat Lake. As a young woman, she met her husband. They married, had a child, and eventually moved to the lighthouse at Cape Beale, on the coast north of modern-day Tofino. Although Thomas was the official lightkeeper, Minnie had an active part in daily operations of the light station. For her heroic rescue, Minnie made headlines in Canada and the United States. She was awarded a framed citation from the Sailor's Union of the Pacific, a silver plate from the Dominion Government, and a silver tea set, golden locket, and cheque from the officers and crew of the coastal steamer *Queen City*.

Nearly a year before Minnie's heroic hike, she accomplished a different rescue. The steamship *Valencia* missed the entrance to the Strait of Juan de Fuca and became shipwrecked on rocks about nine kilometres south of Pachena Point. Survivors got to shore and rang Cape Beale. Minnie took the call, swiftly telegraphing Victoria via Bamfield and Port Alberni with information of the shipwreck. She invited other survivors inside, fed them, and kept them warm in her family's small lightkeeper's quarters.

In 1908, after thirteen years at the Cape Beale lighthouse, Minnie and Thomas moved back to the Alberni Valley. Sadly, Minnie's hike had given her something more sinister than awards and recognition: her body may have been weakened that day, as five years after the trek, she developed tuberculosis and died in 1911. Minnie's story is one of courage, bravery, and dedication. She is remembered as a heroine who saved many lives on Vancouver Island's rugged west coast.

CATHERINE SCHUBERT

Overland Explorer
1835–1918
Cariboo Region, British Columbia

CATHERINE SCHUBERT was the only woman in a group of travellers who travelled from Fort Garry (present-day Winnipeg) to British Columbia in 1862. These "Overlanders," as they were called, hoped to strike it rich at the Cariboo Gold Rush. One hundred and fifty of them tolerated voracious mosquitos, climbed frigid mountain passes, and forded icy rivers on their journey.

Catherine was born in Ireland and moved to the United States at sixteen. She worked as a maid and in her free time, taught herself to read. She married a German carpenter and together they owned a bakery and general store. When their farm flooded, they decided to join the Overlanders and head to the Cariboo Gold Rush.

Catherine brought her three young children (aged five, three, and one) with her on the journey. She rode on horseback, carrying one daughter and one son in each saddle bag, while her husband carried their other son. At first, the other settlers on the journey were resentful that Catherine was there, but they quickly realized she could keep up and hold her own. Catherine was pregnant when the trip began, and went into labour on the six-week rafting segment of the trip while riding a wooden raft down the Thompson River. She pulled to shore and gave birth with the help of some Secwépemc women. The healthy baby girl was named Rose, after the wild rosehips they foraged and ate to survive after losing their canoe.

Four months after leaving Fort Garry, Catherine and her family arrived in British Columbia. This made her the first European woman to enter British Columbia by land. Many Overlanders died on the trip and a disappointing fact awaited Catherine and her family in British Columbia: most of the gold was gone. So they switched their plans from mining to farming. Catherine had two more children and moved to Lillooet, where she worked as a midwife, taught children in her home, and ran an inn and restaurant.

Catherine later moved to Armstrong and lived there until 1918, when she died. In 1934, a Catherine Schubert Memorial cairn was put up in Armstrong, calling her a brave and notable pioneer. Schubert Drive in Kamloops is named after her and her family, and Mount Rose Swanson, a hiking trail in Armstrong, is named after her daughter Rose.

RUTH MASTERS

Mountaineer and Environmental Activist

1920–2017

Courtenay, British Columbia

RUTH MASTERS was a fierce advocate for the lakes, trees, and bears surrounding her beloved town of Courtenay. Born in Comox, BC, in 1920, she lived in a cabin on the Puntledge River without electricity or running water. After college, Ruth assisted in the UK during the Second World War. On her return, she picked fruit, travelled, and worked as a backcountry guide and cook.

Ruth had loved the mountains since hiking Mount Becher at thirteen. She joined the Comox District Mountaineering Club for life. She led hundreds of trips and helped build Strathcona Park's many famous trails.

By day, Ruth worked as a legal secretary, but her passion was wildlife activism. She participated in the 1993 Clayoquot Sound logging blockades and protested the damming of Buttle Lake. She rallied to protect the Price and Thelwood valleys from mining, protected wilderness around Courtenay, and tried to end black bear trophy hunting.

Ruth's community involvement ran far and deep. She helped with search and rescue efforts, was a board member of the Courtenay and District Museum, and was secretary of the Comox District Mountaineering Club. She gave out silver "hero spoons" to citizens who did good deeds. She donated to eighty-five organizations before buying anything extra for herself.

Ruth also loved nature photography, woodwork, and leather work. Three of her leather-bound books are displayed at the Courtenay and District Museum and tell the history of the Comox Valley and Forbidden Plateau.

Some people did not like Ruth and her outspoken ways. Her mailbox was vandalized and she was the subject of her local paper's letters to the editor. In her nineties, Ruth was hauled into a police car and taken away for trying to protect a black bear from police and conservation officers.

In 2004, Ruth donated sixteen acres of land to the Land Conservancy of BC and Comox Valley Land Trust, protecting her family's homestead from logging and development forever. For most of her life, Ruth had lived there with local shelter cats. The Ruth Masters Greenway is located on her donated land and Ruth Masters Lake is in Strathcona Park.

In many ways, Ruth was ahead of her time. She fancied herself an environmental watchdog and encouraged people to act as trustees for the earth. She wanted people to act on their beliefs and believed everyone could make a difference to protect Canada's most valuable treasure—its wilderness.

PHYLLIS MUNDAY

Mountaineering Pioneer
1894–1990
Vancouver, British Columbia

PHYLLIS MUNDAY is one of Vancouver's best-known mountaineering pioneers. She was born in Sri Lanka on a tea plantation where her father, an expatriate British citizen, managed a tea company. In 1901, Phyllis's family moved to Canada, first living in Manitoba, and later Vancouver. There, Phyllis joined the Girl Guides, starting a sixty-year involvement.

Her first ascent was up Grouse Mountain. She was hooked. As a young woman, she worked as a stenographer, but she lived for weekends, which she spent hiking any peak she could: from Mount Bishop to Castle Towers. She canoed to mountains that could only be accessed by lake. This was the early 1900s, when it was highly unusual for women to climb.

Phyllis met her husband Don through friends, and they began mountaineering together. They did a honeymoon hike of Mount Dam on Vancouver's North Shore. In 1918, they were the first people to climb Mount Coquitlam, and in 1920, climbed Mount Robson together. They became known as "the climbing couple." In 1921, Phyllis had a baby she named Edith. At eight weeks old, Edith was taken along on weekend trips, carried in a backpack Phyllis made herself. When they didn't bring Edith, they took turns looking after her. At five years old, Edith was hiking on her own.

In 1923, the family moved to a cabin on Grouse Mountain. It had a wood stove and no running water. Don oversaw the construction of a cabin and tourist lodge while Phyllis cooked for the surveyors and builders and sold concessions to hikers. They lived in the cabin through rain and non-stop snow that they worried would collapse the cabin. Phyllis earned a Bronze Cross medal for valour after saving the life of a boy who fell down the mountain.

Phyllis and Don continued to climb mountains for fun. They were at the forefront of ski-mountaineering after they realized that travelling on skis extended their season and allowed them to travel faster in snowy conditions. Phyllis led Alpine Club of Canada and all-women mountaineering trips, and edited the club's journal. She also had hardships that she mostly kept to herself, like snow blindness and arthritis.

When her arthritis stopped her from hiking, Phyllis accessed the mountains by horseback or plane. Her passion for mountaineering earned her the nickname the "Grand Dame of Mountaineering." Munday Mountain in BC's Coast Mountains is named after her.

FRANCES OLDHAM KELSEY

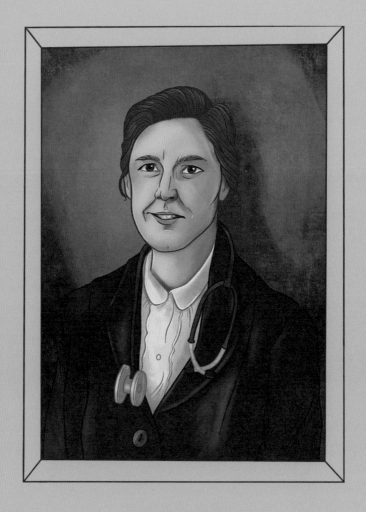

Pharmacologist

1914–2015

Cobble Hill, British Columbia

"FRANKIE," AS SHE was called by friends, family, and colleagues, was born in Cobble Hill, BC. She was the only girl at an all-boys private high school in Shawnigan Lake. After attending St. Margaret's in Victoria, she began an undergraduate degree in zoology at Victoria College, then transferred partway into physiology and pharmocology at McGill. She completed a master's degree in pharmacology, studying the effect of chemicals on the human body. In 1938, she did a doctorate focused on the posterior pituitary gland of armadillos. Frances never wanted to be a doctor; she was interested in research and pharmaceuticals.

While working at the University of Chicago, Frances met another doctor named Ellis Kelsey. They worked on anti-malarial drugs together, eventually married, and had two daughters. Frances later became a medical officer for the US Food and Drug Administration (FDA), reviewing drug applications and ensuring that new drugs on the market were safe for use.

A month into her job, an application for a drug called thalidomide came across Frankie's desk. The pharmaceutical company hailed it as a non-toxic miracle drug that helped pregnant women with morning sickness and sleep. It was already approved for sale in Germany, Canada, and the UK. Frances was immediately concerned, so she delayed the approval for as long as she could. She eventually rejected the application, saying more clinical studies were needed. The drug company pressured Frankie, writing letters, phoning, and visiting her in person to intimidate her. They even tried to have her fired. Frankie held her ground.

As it turned out, Frankie was right to be wary. The drug was found to cause death to unborn babies, or for babies to be born with major birth defects. By 1962, thalidomide was banned worldwide. Frankie saved an estimated 100,000 babies from birth defects, and prevented another 50,000 potential miscarriages. Frankie didn't bask in this victory and never saw herself as deserving fame; she simply saw it as doing her job well.

Frankie was promoted to a Chief Investigator at the FDA and continued as a pharmacologist and pharmacology teacher. She was awarded the President's Award in 1962 by John F. Kennedy, and was inducted into the American National Women's Hall of Fame and given the Order of Canada in 2000. Frances Kelsey Secondary School in Mill Bay is named after her. Frankie's story is one of courage, confidence, and standing up for what you believe is right, no matter the pressure.

HELEN SAWYER HOGG

Astronomer

1905–1993
Victoria, British Columbia

HELEN SAWYER HOGG was passionate about stars. Using a telescope, she studied variable stars and globular clusters—collections of hundreds, thousands, or millions of densely packed stars held together by gravity. They help us estimate the age of the universe and the location of the centre of our galaxy.

Helen was born in Massachusetts and studied astronomy at Mount Holyoke College in Massachusetts. After graduating, she got a job at the Harvard College Observatory and eventually earned her master's degree and doctorate from Radcliffe College. Actually, she rightfully earned them from Harvard, but Harvard didn't grant science degrees to women back then.

Victoria, BC, was Helen's next home, where her husband worked at the Dominion Astrophysical Observatory. A federal government rule disallowed spouses to work there together during Depression years, so Helen wasn't formally employed, but she wasn't deterred. Officially, she became her husband's research assistant, but did her own research.

Helen had a baby, whom she brought along when she did her telescope research. After moving to Toronto, the Hoggs had two more children. Helen did her own research at the David Dunlop Observatory in Richmond Hill, and in 1936, was hired in the astronomy department. She was an assistant professor at the University of Toronto in 1951, associate professor in 1955, and full professor from 1957–76. She wrote a book called *The Stars Belong to Everyone: How to Enjoy Astronomy* and a much-loved weekly column for the *Toronto Star* called "With the Stars" that ran for thirty years.

Helen became known internationally for her studies on stars. Though she didn't have the same opportunities as her husband, she didn't let that stop her. She continued her research unpaid, studying globular clusters and taking photos using the observatory's enormous telescope. She was one of the first female astronomers to use a major research telescope and became known as the "first lady of science."

Helen Sawyer Hogg had a variety of things named after her: an asteroid; the observatory at the Canadian Science and Technology Museum in Ottawa; and an annual lecture by the Royal Astronomical Society of Canada. She received a Medal of Service of the Order of Canada, and was a Fellow of the Royal Society of Canada. Her love of stars remains with us: her photos of variable stars are still cited by astronomers to this day.

VICTORIA CHUNG

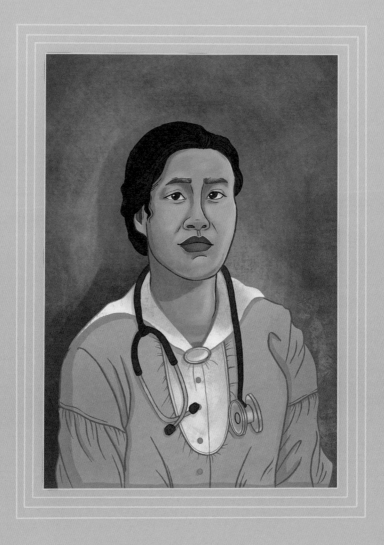

Doctor and Medical Missionary

1897–1966

Victoria, British Columbia

VICTORIA CHUNG achieved her childhood dream of becoming a doctor and medical missionary. She diligently worked toward her goals and became many "firsts," both in British Columbia and Canada: she was the first Chinese Canadian doctor, the first *female* Chinese Canadian doctor, and first female intern at the Toronto General Hospital. Her legacy remains both in Canada, where she was born and raised, and in China, where she spent most of her life working as a surgeon, hospital administrator, and medical missionary.

Victoria's story differs from that of many other missionaries. In her time, many missionaries were male and white; Victoria was female and of Asian descent. Victoria was named after the city in BC where she was born, and Queen Victoria, who was celebrating her Diamond Jubilee that year. Her father, Sing Noon Chung, came to Victoria as a foreign worker in 1881, along with 15,000 other Chinese men who came as construction workers for the transcontinental railway. Victoria's mother Yin Han worked as a midwife, having trained in China.

When Victoria was five or six years old and ready to attend school, her parents enrolled her in kindergarten at the Chinese Rescue Home, later renamed the Oriental Home. Racism was rampant in the city of Victoria during Victoria Chung's childhood. In 1884, the province passed laws that disallowed Chinese people from owning crown land and forced them to pay extra annual taxes. Schools were racially segregated, some businesses refused to hire Chinese employees, and Chinese people were banned from voting and working on public works projects.

After graduating from Victoria High School in 1916, Victoria was awarded a scholarship from the Presbyterian Missionary Society. She applied to and was accepted at the University of Toronto. It was the only medical school in Canada that allowed female students at the time she applied. Although female students were allowed, they endured harassment, sexist chanting from students, and sexist remarks, even from their professors. In 1922, Victoria graduated from medical school and became an intern at Toronto General Hospital—the first woman to do so. In 1923, she wrote her final exams and prepared to go overseas to work as a missionary. The Women's Missionary Society appointed her to the Marion Barclay Hospital for Women and Children in Jiangmen City, China. Victoria had reached her goal, and was a competent and highly valued addition to the hospital. She was a skilled surgeon and was also appointed the hospital's administrator, managing the entire hospital. On top of these major duties, she taught nursing and worked in the hospital's medical dispensary. She accomplished great things for the hospital and the region. Under her direction, the hospital expanded from 33 beds to more than 200. In 1923, her work brought an ambulance to that area of rural southern China, as well as modern hospital equipment, modern medical practices, and medical supplies. Victoria cared for refugees, both at the hospital and in an outreach capacity. She vaccinated against smallpox, typhus, and cholera, and treated for dysentery and malaria. Victoria never gave up on her patients, even if their conditions seemed hopeless. She lived in a residence behind the hospital, which she shared with her friend Dr. Annie Wong and her mother.

In her later years, Victoria brought her medical expertise to remote areas of China that lacked medical care. She is remembered as being a doctor who was professional, skilled, hardworking, and constantly improving. An article in the Peterborough *Examiner* describes Victoria's achievements as a medical missionary: "In five years this efficient Canadian-born woman broke all records for out-patients, in-patients, and confinement cases in her hospital."

She was credited for running a well-equipped, well-led, and modern women's hospital. She constantly fought for the same resources for the women's hospital that existed at the men's hospital. She let nothing get in the way of her goal of becoming a missionary doctor. She was many "firsts," including the first person of Chinese descent—man or woman—to graduate from a medical school in Canada. Victoria Chung is remembered as a medical hero and was certainly a trailblazing woman of Victoria, BC.

JULIA HENSHAW

Botanist and Writer

1869–1937

Vancouver, British Columbia

JULIA HENSHAW had a wide range of talents and interests—botany, photography, writing, mapping, and exploring wild places. She was born in England in 1869 and was educated in France and Germany. In 1890, she moved to Montreal, got married, and had a daughter. In 1891, the family moved to the Lower Mainland of Canada's west coast.

Travelling in the mountains combined two of her passions: botany and climbing. In 1906, her first guidebook, *Mountain Wildflowers of Canada*, was published. It was ahead of its time, replacing lithographs with photos. She even lectured on the flora and fauna of the Canadian Rockies at the International Alpine Congress in Monaco.

Julia loved exploring. In 1910 and 1911, she mapped the interior of Vancouver Island. In 1914, she and her husband were the first people to drive a vehicle across the Rockies. She explored the Kootenay and Columbia Rivers, keeping detailed notes of plants. In 1915, her second guidebook, *Wildflowers of the North American Mountains*, was published. Some said Julia benefitted from the studies of other botanists like Mary Schäffer Warren and got to publishing their work before them.

Along with her other hobbies, Julia was a prolific writer. Her first novel was a romance called *Hypnotized*, published in 1898. It would win the Canadian book of the year. Another novel, *Why Not Sweetheart*, was published in 1901. Julia was editor for the *Vancouver Daily News* from 1900 to 1910. She edited book pages for the *Vancouver Sun* and wrote the *Notebook* column until her death. She penned stories about her mountain climbing adventures in *Overland Monthly*, and about her climbs to the top of the Asulkan Pass. She also published articles for *The Canadian* magazine. To increase her chances of being published and to encourage male readership, Julia wrote using a male "nom de plume"—Julian Durham.

When Julia was forty-five, the First World War broke out. She headed overseas to help with Canada's war effort, driving an ambulance, raising money, and helping with the food units. When she was no longer able to climb mountains, she continued writing, lecturing, and studying botany.

Julia was a founding member of the Alpine Club of Canada, the Georgian Club, and the Woman's Musical Club. Henshaw Creek in Strathcona Park is named after her. Her legacy includes guidebooks, writing, and exploration.

EDITH BERKELEY

Marine Biologist
1875–1963
Nanaimo, British Columbia

IN 1919, Edith Berkeley arrived in the coal mining town of Nanaimo, BC, to study marine worms. Despite having a degree in zoology from London University, she was not permitted to be on the staff of the Pacific Biological Station in Departure Bay, and had to settle instead for being a volunteer investigator. Edith was a scientist and professor before it was common for women to do either; she was undaunted by her demotion. In many ways, being a volunteer afforded her more freedom than being a staff member. She could do research and field work and publish her work freely, despite being married, while paid female staff members were expected to stop working if they married. She made the absolute most of her opportunities; in fact, she became a world authority on marine polychaetes (marine worms).

Edith was born in South Africa to English parents. As a teenager, she travelled solo from Tasmania to England around Cape Horn. She was headed to London University to pursue a scholarship in pre-medical studies, although partway through she switched to chemistry and zoology.

There, Edith met a fellow scientist, Cyril Berkeley. They married in 1902 and moved to Bihar, India, after graduation. In 1903, they had a daughter. They lived and worked in India for twelve years until the monsoons became too much to bear.

In 1914, the couple moved to BC's Okanagan Valley. There, they farmed a ranch and taught at the newly founded University of British Columbia. Edith taught zoology and Cyril, bacteriology. Eventually they came to a realization: they were good ranchers, but their hearts were in research.

In 1919, they moved again, this time to Nanaimo, where they both started doing research—albeit Edith as a volunteer, leaving a paid, dependable position as a professor but following her passion. She published 12 research papers as sole author and 34 jointly with Cyril. She revelled in never-before-studied worms—some from depths of up to nearly five kilometres. Her research put the Pacific Biological Station on the map and contributed to its reputation.

Edith conducted research until the end of her life. Her talent and passion were admirable and inspiring, paving the way for future female marine biologists. Several species are named in her honour, including the Berkeley eualid or Berkeley's shrimp (*Eualus berkeleyorum*), a small red shrimp with a bent tail and distinct bands around its abdomen.

EMMA STARK

Pioneer Teacher
1856–1890
Nanaimo, British Columbia

IN 1858, eight hundred African Americans arrived on the Saanich peninsula and moved to various locations on Vancouver Island and the Gulf Islands. Several dozen went to Salt Spring Island, including Sylvia and Louis Stark. Sylvia's father was born into slavery in Missouri and eventually bought his and his family's freedom. Louis, too, had been born into slavery, and had also bought his freedom. Sylvia and Louis met in California and married. One of their five children was Emma Arabella Stark.

The Starks eventually moved to the Cranberry area of Nanaimo, except for their son, who stayed on Salt Spring Island. They valued education and sent Emma and her sister Marie to the closest school over thirteen kilometres away in Cedar. Back then, it was common for students who lived far away to stay near the school during the week. Sylvia would bring the girls home on weekends by horseback. In winter, they travelled in a hand-built ox-drawn sled. Eventually, Sylvia moved to a farm on Salt Spring Island, joining her son, Willis. Emma and her father remained in Nanaimo.

Despite the tragic passing of her father, Emma finished high school and in 1874, aged eighteen, became the first Black schoolteacher on Vancouver Island. She taught at the new Cedar-Cranberry school, a one-room schoolhouse that students travelled from far and wide to attend, until 1879, earning $40 a month. Emma was a competent teacher and well-liked by students.

In 1878, Emma married James Clark in Victoria. After that, little is known of her life. She died aged only thirty-three, of an unknown cause. She is buried in Salt Spring Island next to her grandfather. Emma's mother Sylvia later became a prominent personality on Salt Spring Island.

Sylvia's and Emma's stories are ones of freedom and self-determination. Sylvia made a long journey to freedom, while Emma endured the many hardships so typical of pioneer life, but also passed on the gift of knowledge to her students. They were welcomed into the community and did not experience the discrimination that they had faced previously. Today, the Stark farm's barn still stands on Extension Road, beside Chase River Elementary School. Stark Lake, in Nanaimo's Extension area, and Stark Landing, where the railroad passed the family orchard and cattle fields, are named after the family. A plaque in downtown Nanaimo bears Emma's name, honouring her as "the first Black teacher on Vancouver Island."

KIMIKO MURAKAMI

Farmer and Internment Camp Survivor

1904–1997

Salt Spring Island, British Columbia

GANBARU MEANS "persevere" in Japanese. Kimiko Murakami maintained a *ganbaru* mentality during a time of appalling injustices to Japanese Canadians.

Kimiko was born in Steveston, but moved to Salt Spring Island with her family when she was five. Japanese Canadians were not permitted to vote or work in certain professions at that time, but they could fish, farm, and log. From a young age, Kimiko would deliver fish by boat to Vancouver.

Kimiko and her sister attended school and looked after their siblings while her parents fished. The family business was successful, but they eventually sold the boats and bought farmland. Kimiko's father built Salt Spring Island's first greenhouse and grew high-quality produce. Eventually, Kimiko bought her own farm with her husband.

Everything changed when Japan bombed Pearl Harbour on December 7, 1941. Japanese Canadians became viewed as "enemy aliens" and a security risk to Canada. They faced daily racism and attacks. On February 26, 1942, the War Measures Act barred Japanese Canadians from a 161-kilometre area along the coast. Government officials seized assets and interned Japanese Canadians, many of them born in Canada. About 22,000 Japanese Canadians in BC were interned in camps east of the Rockies.

Kimiko and her five children were taken to Hastings Camp, where the Pacific National Exhibition and Playland stands today in Vancouver. They lived in bitterly cold animal barracks with no indoor toilets or water. Then they were transferred to a camp in Greenwood, BC. They shared one filthy cubicle in a crowded bunkhouse. Later, they were moved to Magrath, Alberta, where they were forced to work at a sugar beet farm.

After the war, Japanese Canadians were again allowed to move, vote, and access rights as Canadian citizens. Kimiko and her family returned to Salt Spring Island, the only Japanese-Canadian family to do so. Their land had been sold without their consent. Kimiko didn't give up; she bought scrubland on Rainbow Road and built a farm business all over again. Again, they worked hard farming and growing high-quality food.

Kimiko's portrait hangs on the wall of the National Archives of Canada. She endured human rights atrocities and filthy internment camps, but she retained pride, hope, and integrity, refusing to become bitter and hateful. Kimiko never gave up, always did her best, and held on, embodying the true meaning of the word *ganbaru*.

ANNA PETROVNA MARKOVA

Doukhobor Pioneer

1902–1978

Castlegar, British Columbia

ANNA PETROVNA MARKOVA came to British Columbia after being released from a labour camp, or gulag, in Soviet Russia. Although Anna was innocent, she spent fifteen years in the gulag because of her Doukhobor faith. Many people died there, but Anna survived. She was released in the 1950s and allowed to move to Canada in 1960 with help from prominent people like Eleanor Roosevelt.

Much of her family, who were Doukhobor leaders, had died or already moved to Canada. Doukhobors are a pacifist religious sect who were persecuted in Russia for separating from the Russian Eastern Orthodox Church and refusing military service. Large numbers left Russia in 1899, with 7,500 coming to Canada. They initially settled in the prairies in Saskatchewan, but between 1908 and 1913, almost 6,000 moved west to the Kootenays in BC. Many established a communal enterprise called Brilliant, near Castlegar.

Despite harsh labour camp conditions and losing her husband, brother, and son while imprisoned, Anna didn't live in anger. She became a leader and activist, committed to making life better for her community—especially women and children. Anna rallied and led other women to raise funds for less fortunate community members. They made blankets, linen, cookbooks, and wooden crafts to be sold. They also fundraised to build the Brilliant Cultural Centre—a multi-use facility open to all to celebrate Doukhobor faith and culture. They made and sold *lapsha*, homemade Russian noodles, and *pyrahi*, Russian tarts with vegetarian fillings like peas and beans. Today, the Brilliant Cultural Centre remains a vibrant hub for Doukhobor culture and hosts many community events. Anna led efforts to establish Verigin Memorial Park, a Doukhobor flower garden and burial site where revered Doukhobor leaders like Anna's parents, son, and Anna herself, now rest.

Anna also celebrated her faith and culture through song. Many said she sang like a professional. In 1978, she co-compiled and co-edited a book on Doukhobor psalms, hymns, and songs. She also recorded many songs.

Anna is honoured in her community. There's room with her name in the Doukhobor Discovery Centre, and a TV documentary outlines her forgiveness in exile. Markova Road in Castlegar is named for her.

Forgiveness for those who imposed suffering on her and her family and promoting peace were focuses of Anna's life. She was determined to live in hope and generosity rather than anger and hatred.

ISABELLA MAINVILLE ROSS

Landowner

1808–1885

Victoria, British Columbia

MANY ON Vancouver Island know of Ross Bay Cemetery, but fewer know of the woman who once farmed the land where the cemetery sits. This woman was Isabella Mainville Ross, and she was the first female registered landowner in what is now British Columbia.

Isabella was born on January 10, 1808, likely near modern-day Fort Frances, Ontario. Her mother was Ojibway and her father was French and Spanish. In 1822, Isabella married Charles George Ross, a boatman for the Hudson's Bay Company. The couple moved from Fort Frances to Fort Vancouver and then to Fort McLoughlin—a fur trade outpost on Campbell Island near modern-day Bella Bella. There, when Isabella was trading on behalf of her husband, who was away, a man pulled a knife on her son. Isabella grabbed a knife of her own, charged at the man, and chased him out of the fort.

The family's final move was to Fort Victoria, in 1843. Charles was promoted to Chief Trader for the HBC, and was in charge of supervising the construction of Fort Victoria. He died suddenly, leaving Isabella widowed at thirty-six years old, with nine children, including a newborn, a toddler, and three children under ten. They moved to Fort Nisqually near Puget Sound, Washington, where they lived for eight years.

The family eventually moved back to Victoria and, with money left to her in Charles's will, Isabella purchased ninety-nine acres of land. This acquisition was significant and historic for several reasons. It made her the first female landowner, and likely the first Indigenous person, to own land under colonial law in what is now British Columbia. Isabella named her property Fowl Bay Farm, after the area's waterfowl.

Isabella's children attended school while she worked the land. Isabella sold livestock and farm produce. Though she couldn't read or write English, she spoke French, Ojibway, and likely Chinook Jargon, a language used for trade. All her children lived to be adults—an unusual occurrence in days of high infant mortality rates and rampant disease.

A tall, handsome headstone in Ross Bay Cemetery bears Isabella's name, on the very land where she used to grow potatoes and raise livestock. She was the first woman to own land on Vancouver Island and a prominent Victoria woman whose name will remain in the city where she lived her pioneer life.

MARIA MAHOI

Sailor and Midwife

1855–1936
Russell Island, British Columbia

MARIA MAHOI was a woman of the water. She loved the ocean and being in the water, and spent her life on islands. Water was her constant companion, and a persistent acquaintance through every stage of her life. Maria was a pioneer who left an impression on her island homes for her resourcefulness and strength of spirit.

Maria's story begins in Victoria, where many Hawaiian people arrived after leaving their tropical island homes. Hawaiian people came to BC's west coast to work for the Hudson's Bay Company, or for the California Gold Rush.

Maria was likely born in Fort Victoria. Her father was Hawaiian and her mother was Coast Salish. Maria and her first husband Abel lived together in Fort Victoria and later moved to Pasley Island, west of Bowen Island. Maria learned to sail aboard Abel's forty-foot schooner. They later moved to Salt Spring Island, where they acquired over 100 acres of land near Beaver Point for farming. They had seven children and farmed and fished.

Maria worked as a midwife, eventually remarried, and had six more children. Some good fortune came in 1902: William Haumea, a well-known Hawaiian patriarch that some said was Maria's father, died and left Maria his house and property on nearby Russell Island. Maria would go out deer-hunting, often with a child strapped to her back. She mended her children's clothing, wove clothes from sheep's wool, and carefully preserved food from their gardens and orchards.

Years passed and Maria's children grew up. They got married, became educated, and had their own children, whom Maria helped bring into the world as a midwife. One of her sons fought in the First World War, hiding his Indigenous ancestry in order to serve. Her older sons became sealers. And despite living remotely, Maria was not socially isolated. She nourished many female friendships and often rowed her boat to Salt Spring Island to visit them. She loved paddling her canoe, sailing, and swimming.

Maria Mahoi was strong in body and spirit. She remained tough and resilient through a challenging time in history, living through turbulent politics and rampant racism against anyone who wasn't the dominant race. She was exceptional at doing more with less. Islands were her home and the ocean her playmate, confidante, and life spirit. A prominent "Kanaka matriarch," she lived a captivating and fulsome life.

MARY ANN GYVES/ TUWA´HWIYE TUSIUM GOSSELIM

Homestead Midwife
1854–1941
Salt Spring Island, British Columbia

MARY ANN GYVES, or Tuwa'hwiye Tusium Gosselim, was born at Burgoyne Bay, a sparkling cove between the mouths of two creeks on Salt Spring Island's western shore. In Hul'qumi'num, Burgoyne Bay is called "Hwaaqw'um," or "place of the sawbill ducks." It boasted clam beds, herring, streams teeming with Coho and chum salmon, sawbill ducks, and camas fields.

Mary Ann was one of three children. Her father was George Tusilum, a Cowichan Chieftain; her mother, a daughter of the L'uml'umluts Clan, was named Taltunaat. As a girl, Mary Ann collected local plants—including salmonberries, button-berries, and Oregon grape shoots—in a woven cedar basket. A healer from a young age, she learned midwifery from her Cowichan family and would later deliver many babies on Salt Spring Island.

In July 1886, Mary Ann married Michael Gyves, one of Salt Spring Island's original settlers. They purchased land and began building a homestead together. The forest was extremely dense and had to be cleared before the land could be farmed. To clear the land, Mary Ann tied tree stumps to a plow with chains. Michael drove the plow until the stumps were removed from the ground, while Mary Ann led the oxen that pulled the plow. A stoneboat (a sled-like box) was used to haul away rocks. They saved wood to build barns, houses, and fences.

Their land had many giant cedar trees several metres in diameter, and Mary Ann and Michael went into business making cedar shakes (roofing shingles) from them. There were no roads to get the shakes to the water and no wharves. In fact, at this point, there were no roads at all on the island. Michael would row the shakes to Sidney or Victoria to be sold at markets.

Mary Ann had three children, Ellen, Michael, and Mary Katherine. She kept her Catholic faith but also maintained her Indigenous culture, teaching her children and grandchildren her culture and the Hul'qumi'num language.

Mary Ann lived and worked the land on Salt Spring Island long before the island had ferry service, before the iconic Mouat's store opened up, before the island was logged, before Mount Maxwell had its name, and before the island became a hip destination known for its farmer's markets.

NELLIE YIP QUONG

Midwife, Public Health Nurse, and Activist
1882–1949
Vancouver, British Columbia

NELLIE YIP QUONG was an outspoken advocate for Chinese Canadian women at a time when anti-Chinese racism was rampant in Vancouver. She was white, but fought against injustices toward Chinese Canadians, especially in health care. She had a part in changing hospital policies that confined Chinese patients and other racialized patients to the basement. Nellie was also a midwife, feminist, and public health nurse.

Nellie was born in Saint John, New Brunswick. She attended private school and moved to New York City to teach English. There, she met Charles Yip Quong, a jeweller from Vancouver. They fell in love and got married. After living in China for a few years, they moved to Vancouver's Chinatown. Established in the 1880s, it was one of the oldest and largest in Canada at the time.

Nellie worked as a public health nurse for the Chinese Benevolent Association of Vancouver. From the early 1900s to the 1930s, Nellie provided health and social services to immigrant Chinese women and their families. Many of these women were especially vulnerable as they had not been encouraged to learn English, or due to their jobs as servants or waitresses. Nellie helped them navigate social services, translated for court cases, and helped with issues with employers, landlords, and immigration officials. She cared for the elderly and helped deliver hundreds of babies as a midwife. She had one adopted daughter of her own.

Nellie was especially helpful as an advocate because she spoke five different Chinese dialects. She helped women in their own language. She helped immigrants work with Canadian authorities and helped workers know their rights. She even demanded that a restaurant take down a sign that was racist toward Chinese and Indigenous Peoples.

Nellie became known as "Granny Yip" or "Granny." She is recognized as a National Historic Person of Significance in Canada. A meeting room in the Strathcona branch of the Vancouver Public Library is named after her, and a plaque in Vancouver commemorates her. Nellie is remembered as a midwife and interpreter.

BARBARA TOUCHIE/ SIČQUUʔUƛ

Language Champion

1931–2014

Ucluelet, British Columbia

FOR THE first years of her life, Barbara Touchie, also known as Sičquuʔuƛ, spoke only the Barkley dialect of the Nuu-chah-nulth language. Although she would learn English and speak it throughout the rest of her life, she always remained fluent in Nuu-chah-nulth and passed her knowledge of the language on to thousands of people.

Barbara was a language champion. If you've been to Tofino or Ucluelet, maybe you've visited Parks Canada's Kwisitis Visitor Centre on Wickaninnish Beach in Pacific Rim National Park. Barbara was instrumental in the inclusion of Nuu-chah-nulth linguistic and cultural content there, and the richness this language and culture adds to this visitor centre is still visible today. Barbara spent years of her life revitalizing the Barkley dialect of the Nuu-chah-nulth language and making it accessible to the hundreds of thousands of tourists visiting the area she always called home.

Barbara was born in Opitsaht (across from Tofino on Meares Island) in 1931. Her mother was Ella Thompson and her father was Joe Thompson. Barbara was the youngest and only girl of five children. Her four older brothers were forced to attend residential school, but Barbara's parents refused to let her be taken. Barbara spent her earliest years in Tofino and was later sent to live with her grandfather, Toquaht Jim, in Ucluelet. Her brothers were much older than her and had moved away to find work. Barbara spent the rest of her childhood in Hakoda Bay, now known as Stewart Bay, where her grandfather owned a small property. There were no roads connecting Ucluelet to the rest of Vancouver Island at this time. People lived off the land and sea; essentials were picked up in Port Alberni by boat.

After Barbara's coming of age, she married a man her mother chose for her. Barbara was one of the last women in her community to have an arranged marriage, which, in her culture, involved a woman's mother choosing a husband she found suitable for her daughter. Samuel Touchie was the man Barbara's mother chose, and she was confident that he would be a virtuous husband. And as it turned out, she was right! Barbara and Sam's eldest daughter, Vi Mundy, remembers her parents having a solid partnership. They had fifteen children, eight daughters and seven sons, that they raised together. They both had the same ideas about parenting and never once argued in front of their children. Family teachings included respecting oneself and one's elders, listening with the heart, helping one another, especially Elders, getting up early, being involved in the community, helping with activities and clean up at community gatherings, helping at home, learning to cook, and other basic life skills. The children were taught to be independent and not rely on others to take care of them. Sam also supported Barbara in working outside of the home—not a common decision for a woman at that time.

Barbara's work included sitting on the council for the Ucluelet First Nation and being involved in housing and setting up a membership code for Nation members. Her work also largely involved language, much of which was done when she was between 65 and 83 years old. In the 1990s, she and several other women developed an alphabet for the Barkley dialect of the Nuu-chah-nulth language. Barbara worked with Parks Canada to make Nuu-chah-nulth language and culture visible to the hundreds of thousands of tourists who visit Tofino and Ucluelet annually. She played a major role in updates to the Kwisitis Visitor Centre, making sure the Nuu-chah-nulth People's history, language, and culture was represented there. She worked on translating the David Suzuki Foundation's values—the Declaration of Interdependence—into Nuu-chah-nulth. Challenges she faced through her life included major changes in society over the years, the passing of her husband, and the passing of some of her children in her later years.

Barbara passed away in 2014 at the age of 83. As a key person in the preservation and revitalization of Nuu-chah-nulth culture and language, Barbara Touchie left a strong legacy. With her cultural and linguistic knowledge and strength of spirit, she was able to preserve, teach, and share the Nuu-chah-nulth language. In turn, this made it possible for others to further preserve the traditions, knowledge, and wisdom of the Nuu-chah-nulth people within the language and pass it on to thousands of people. Barbara's name lives on. She is honoured at language ceremonies, including the "Let the Languages Live" conference in Victoria, BC, that celebrated 2019 as the International Year of Indigenous Languages.

A Parks Canada exhibit is dedicated to her and in 2005, they held a celebration honouring her by naming a theatre after her. Barbara's voice literally lives on as one of the voices heard on the First Voices Indigenous language app, for the Barkley dialect of the Nuu-chah-nulth language. Even now, Barbara is still teaching.

ANN ELMORE HAIG-BROWN

Activist and Librarian
1908–1990
Campbell River, British Columbia

ANN HAIG-BROWN loved books and nature from a young age. She achieved the highest possible scores in the University of Washington's psychology program and attended Berkeley for an Arts degree. After university, Ann worked in a well-known bookstore. It was there she met Roderick Haig-Brown, a writer from England. They exchanged books and letters for three years. When they eventually got engaged, their letters discussed wedding plans and designs for their house, garden, and married life.

Moving to Campbell River, they lived off money from Roderick's writing, and ate from their garden. Then Roderick got drafted for the Second World War. With him gone, Ann had to do the work of two people, maintaining the house and gardens, and raising the children, now aged seven, five, and two. She adjusted her life and got on with it, waking up earlier in the morning and enlisting the children for chores. A former city girl, Ann was now a full-fledged homesteader living in an island wilderness, raising three kids on her own.

Ann was a key person in her community, even when Roderick was away. She canvassed for the Red Cross, and was a Scout leader and a member of the Catholic Women's League, Voice of Women, Parent-Teacher Association, and Campbell River Recreational Association.

Ann also had a major part in the thirty-one books that Roderick wrote. She would type and re-type manuscripts, this being before copy machines existed. Like so many women of her time, she is an unsung heroine.

Ann's guest room often hosted local women who needed a safe place to sleep. In 1959, Ann started working at the high school in Campbell River, eventually becoming librarian and making the library the pride and joy of the school. In her later years, she helped with the library at a women's safe house. The women and their children called her "Granny Ann." She was known for being a gifted listener. Later in life, she was involved in the Cystic Fibrosis Society of BC, Friends of Schizophrenics, and Kingfisher Creek Ecological Reserve—a protected area near her property.

Ann's name has been applied to a mountain, a cabin at a wilderness lodge, and her beloved homestead. The Ann Elmore Transition House opened in 1987 to provide a safe place for women and children fleeing abusive situations. Open still, it offers a variety of support options for individuals. In 2008, the mayor of Campbell River declared May 3 Ann Elmore Day.

ALMA RUSSELL

Librarian, Archivist, and Preserver of History
1873–1964
Victoria, British Columbia

AFTER COMPLETING high school in the late 1800s, Alma Russell left her hometown of Victoria, British Columbia, for New York City. Born in the Maritimes and raised in Victoria, she sought higher education in New York.

She studied at the Pratt Institute of Library Sciences in Brooklyn and upon graduating, was offered at job in New York City. She turned it down and returned to Victoria. Within the year, she was offered a job as librarian and archivist at the Legislative Library. It was 1897, and Alma Russell had become British Columbia's first professionally educated librarian—woman or man.

Alma got straight to work cataloguing and classifying thousands of books in the library. Although community members could access the library, Members of Legislative Assembly (MLAs) were the most frequent patrons. Despite her expertise and recent education, Alma wasn't paid adequately and didn't obtain full-time work. But she persevered. She created a system for archives to be searched using catalogue cards. Her library was the first in BC to use the Dewey decimal system—a library classification system that shelves books with others of the same subject.

Preserving history was part of Alma's job and one she took seriously. She lovingly looked after the Pacific Northwest History collection and created a wartime memorial project of her own. The project was an extensive collection of letters and photos from BC soldiers of the First World War.

Alma often spoke and wrote about British Columbia's history. She was the first woman to be president of the BC Historical Association. She also served as vice president and then president of the BC Library Association.

In New York, Alma had learned about the Travelling Libraries program. She started one on Vancouver Island, successfully delivering reading materials into the hands of farmers, miners, and people living in Vancouver Island's far-off nooks and crannies. This was in a time before public libraries existed.

Throughout her career, Alma wasn't given the credit she deserved. It was only when she came out of retirement in 1934 that she was granted the title of provincial librarian and archivist. She hadn't been given it before, because she was a woman. Today, two islands off Ucluelet bear Alma Russell's name.

SARA ELLEN SPENCER

Philanthropist and Businesswoman
1885–1983
Victoria, British Columbia

DESPITE HER contributions to the City of Victoria, few people have heard of Sara Ellen Spencer. Sara was a philanthropist who contributed greatly to the city of Victoria and spent much of her time and energy helping others.

Sara was one of thirteen children from an English mother and Welsh father. She grew up in Victoria. She rode horses and was part of the first class of Victoria College held in Craigdarroch Castle. Her father owned one of Canada's first department stores—David Spencer Ltd. with locations in Victoria and Greater Vancouver. Sara was on the board of directors of the Victoria store and the Victoria *Daily Times* from 1946 to 1948.

Sara served in leadership roles for various charities, including the Red Cross, Community Chest Drive, and Victoria Women's Voluntary Services. She was president of the Victoria Symphony Society. During the First World War, she served overseas as second-in-command with the Canada Field Comforts Commission and was awarded the Order of the British Empire.

The arts were Sara's true passion. She did all she could to promote the arts in Victoria. She was president of the Victoria Arts Board and vice-president and lifetime honorary vice-president of the art gallery's board of directors.

In 1949, Sara founded the Sara Spencer Foundation; its purpose was to build and manage affordable office space for small health and social services agencies. In 1951, she donated her house to the city to be used as an art gallery. The house, known as the Spencer Mansion, was an elegant Victorian style house located near Craigdarroch Castle on Moss Street. Some people didn't want the Spencer Mansion turned to an art gallery for property tax reasons, but the provincial government provided grants, and the Victoria Arts Centre formally opened on October 15, 1952. A sketch of Sara Ellen Spencer painted by her niece stands by the entrance.

Sara was awarded the BC Centennial Senior Citizen medal in 1958 and made an Honorary Citizen of the City of Victoria in the 1970s. She left an unforgettable legacy, impacting Victoria's commercial, cultural, political, and humanitarian life. Artists in Victoria had sought an art gallery venue for years; Sara's donation of the Spencer mansion made it possible.

GA'AXSTA'LAS/
JANE CONSTANCE COOK

Activist and Interpreter
1870–1951
Alert Bay, British Columbia

G A'AXSTA'LAS, or Jane Constance Cook, was a midwife, a political activist for land and women's rights, a mediator, translator, interpreter, and mother of sixteen children. She used her education and language skills to fiercely advocate for her family and community.

Ga'axsta'las was born in Port Blakely on Bainbridge Island, in Puget Sound. Her mother was a high-ranking first-born Kwakwaka'wakw woman, and her father was an English sailor. In 1879, the same year the Indian Act was passed and gave the government extensive control over Indigenous Peoples' lives, Ga'axsta'las arrived in Alert Bay. She attended and survived the Indian Girls' Mission residential school.

In 1888, Ga'axsta'las married Stephen Cook. They made the unusual and controversial decision to leave the Potlatch system, which was primarily, but not exclusively, aimed at redistributing community wealth. Ga'axsta'las disagreed with the custom of getting married multiple times for the sake of bringing wealth and prestige to a woman's family. She believed Potlatches gave men elevated status and wealth while the well-being of women and children was not considered and they were left with limited options. She didn't agree with underaged girls being married without their consent, and wanted women to have a right to choose their partner and have a say in their own marriages.

Ga'axsta'las's ability to speak both English and Kwak'wala, at a time when there were many court hearings and political shifts, put her in a unique and powerful position. From 1910 onwards, she not only interpreted in court, but also translated and interpreted speeches and church sermons.

Her involvement in the community was far-reaching. She spoke out against tuberculosis hospitals, campaigned for nonracist health services, translated powerful Chiefs' words on land rights, and fought for support for destitute women and children. She also spoke out against proposed reductions in reserve lands and fought for better access to education for her people; for timber, food, hunting and fishing rights.

Ga'axsta'las dedicated her life to fighting for women to have social, political, and economic equity. Living in a Eurocentric, male-dominated society, she frequently stood up to very powerful white men—politicians, police chiefs, Indian Affairs officials, missionaries, and bishops. She spoke for the most vulnerable people of her community when they most needed a voice.

EVELYN PENROSE

Water Diviner

c. 1900–c. 1970

Kamloops, British Columbia

E VELYN PENROSE had a highly unusual job. She was a water diviner, finding water underground using a forked stick or her hands. Evelyn also believed she could find oil, gas, precious metals, gold, and even illness in the body.

Evelyn was born in England and claimed that she came from a long line of water diviners. She lost both her parents at a young age, and as a young girl, learned to use a forked hazel or willow stick, called a "divining rod," to find water. Water divining was also called water witching or water dowsing. In her twenties, she went to visit an uncle in California. It was there that she discovered her abilities to locate oil.

After California, Evelyn went to Hawaii, then BC's Okanagan Valley, where drought was ravishing the land. She was hired by BC's finance minister as the province's first water diviner. Droughts were a big problem in the interior in the 1920s and '30s, but Evelyn didn't disappoint. She found streams running six feet underground with enough water to irrigate the dying orchards and thirsty farms. Evelyn divined for gold in Kamloops, but returned to Victoria after a mine tunnel collapsed and she thought it could be cursed.

To find whatever substance she was seeking, Evelyn used a weight hanging from a stick as a pendulum, a forked hazel stick, or her hands. She described a feeling like a rope pulling her toward her target. Divining wasn't easy—it took a physical toll on Evelyn, causing nausea and headaches. She said she didn't learn the craft, but that it was a natural part of who she was. Later in her career, she could find water or minerals with her hands only. She was sometimes hired to find springs on private land and could even divine minerals from maps. Evelyn's work in the Okanagan, Cariboo, and Peace regions of BC during the 1930s earned her the name the "Divine Lady."

Later, Evelyn went abroad, working in France, England, Hawaii, South Africa, Chile, and Jamaica. Though she believed she could find criminals with her powers, she avoided this for her own safety.

Evelyn wrote a book called *Adventure Unlimited: A Water Diviner Travels the World*. Though water divining was controversial and some believed it to be fake, Evelyn Penrose never doubted herself. She saw herself as a triumphant heroine of her own life story. She always claimed she didn't just exist, but really lived!

MARTHA BLACK

Politician, Botanist, and Pioneer
1866–1957
Dawson City and Whitehorse, Yukon

MARTHA BLACK became known as the "First Lady of the Yukon." She was a brave pioneer with a passion for wildflowers and politics. Martha was determined and feisty from a young age. Born in Chicago to a wealthy family, she went to private school in Indiana. She got married and headed to the gold rush with her husband in 1898. On the way, her husband bailed, but Martha carried on. On the long and arduous journey, she realized she was pregnant. Once in Dawson, she lived with her brother in a one-bedroom cabin with tree trunk furniture, sewing baby clothes by candlelight from lace tablecloths.

They nearly ran out of food that winter, but her son was born healthy. To give birth without a husband was highly unconventional back then, but Martha didn't care. After Martha survived the massive 1899 Dawson fire, she returned briefly to her parents' ranch in Kansas, but quickly became bored and returned to the Yukon, saying she preferred "liberty and opportunity" over "shelter and safety."

Martha was managing a sawmill when she met a lawyer named George Black. They married in 1904 and had a life of camping trips, meaningful work, social events, and family. When Dawson City got too small for George's law practice, the family moved to Vancouver.

Martha had always loved spring flora in the Klondike and mounted wildflowers on watercolour paper. Her "artistic botany" wasn't truly noticed until 1924, when she was commissioned to make pieces for the Canadian Pacific Railway's stations and hotels. She was made a Fellow of the Royal Geographical Society for her research on Yukon flora. Martha also went to Europe for three years, working in the Public Works departments, sewing for the Red Cross, visiting wounded Yukon soldiers in hospital, and writing for two Yukon papers.

Martha supported George during his four terms as a federal MP for the Yukon. When he retired in 1935, Martha ran successfully in his place, just shy of her seventieth birthday. She served for five years, fiercely advocating for her constituents. She was remembered as a charismatic and confident MP.

In 1940, Martha wrote a memoir called *My Ninety Years*. She lived in the Yukon until her death in 1957, leaving an indelible mark on a place she deeply treasured. A Canadian coast guard ship is named after her and she was awarded the Order of the British Empire in 1948. Nobody had frontier spirit like Martha Black.

ROSEMARY BROWN

Brown is Beautiful

Politician, Professor, and Activist
1930–2003
Vancouver, British Columbia

ROSEMARY BROWN was an outspoken advocate for women of colour in Canada. She was a politician, professor, and champion for social justice and women's rights, the first Black woman to win a seat in a provincial legislature.

Rosemary was born in Jamaica in 1930. She attended McGill University in Montreal, where she was discriminated against by roommates, other students, landlords, and even potential employers for being Black. After her degree, she married and moved to Vancouver. She had three children and fought against racism with other members of the BC Association for Advancement of Coloured Peoples. She then went back to school to become a social worker, founding the Vancouver Status of Women Council to fight for equal rights for men and women, and encourage other women of colour to do the same. She wanted the feminist movement to be for everyone—no matter their skin colour.

Rosemary's political career began when she was asked by the provincial New Democratic Party to run in the next election. She said yes, and in 1972, made Canadian history when she was elected to the BC Legislature. She held her seat in the Vancouver-Burrard riding for fourteen years, and helped introduce laws that prohibited discrimination due to marital status and gender. She was a member of the Security Intelligence Review Committee, a watchdog for the Canadian Security Intelligence Service. She helped pass provincial human rights laws and helped BC become the first province to fund women's shelters.

After this, Rosemary became professor of women's studies at Simon Fraser University. She fought to rid Canadian textbooks of racism and sexism. In 1975, Rosemary was the first woman to run for leadership of a federal political party, with the slogan "Brown is Beautiful." Although she lost, she kept fighting for her beliefs and was later a chief commissioner of the Ontario Human Rights Commission, as well as the executive director of MATCH International Centre, which helps women in developing countries.

Rosemary was highly respected for her work and insights. She was awarded a lifetime member of the Privy Council of Canada, received Orders of BC and Canada, won a United Nations Human Rights Fellowship and earned fifteen honorary Doctorates of Law from prestigious Canadian universities. She is remembered to this day through an annual award that recognizes women or organizations fighting for social justice and equality—things Rosemary championed all her life.

BARBARA HOWARD

Sprinter and Teacher
1920–2017
Vancouver, British Columbia

BARBARA HOWARD was the first Black female athlete to represent Canada internationally. She was a fast sprinter who pushed limits and broke records. She was also the first person of colour to teach with the Vancouver School Board.

Barbara was born and raised in Vancouver. She was the youngest of four children. In high school, she started running track, and her talent and speed were immediately evident. In grade eleven, at seventeen years old, she ran 100 yards in 11.2 seconds. In 1938, she competed on the Canadian national track team. This earned her a spot representing Canada at the 1938 British Empire Games in Sydney, Australia. It took her a month by boat to get there. She placed sixth in the 100-yard dash, and also ran for the Canadian relay team. After the race, she became a minor celebrity, even making the front-page news. The Tokyo Olympics would have been her next race, but the Second World War prevented them from happening. Unfortunately, the Tokyo Olympics weren't rescheduled, which meant Barbara's sprinting career was over. Barbara didn't stay down about this, though, and turned her focus to teaching.

Her first teaching position was teaching physical education at Lord Strathcona Elementary School in Vancouver. In 1948, there were few to no people of colour working as teachers in her school district. She taught physical education for fourteen years. She worked tirelessly to engage students and inspire them to reach their full potential. She believed in success for all students, and that the child was more important than the curriculum. She coached volleyball and baseball and learned folk dancing from her Ukrainian students. She was involved in Canadian Girls in Training, an organization similar to Girl Guides that helped girls go to camp and learn leadership and social responsibility.

The Vancouver Park Board awarded Barbara with the Remarkable Woman Award in 2010. In 2012, she was inducted into the BC Sports Hall of Fame, and in 2015, into Canada's Sports Hall of Fame. In 2018, the Cambie Street Plaza in Vancouver was renamed the Barbara Howard Plaza. Barbara Howard is remembered as a Canadian sports legend.

LOIS SMITH

Ballerina

1929–2011

Gibsons, British Columbia

LOIS SMITH is one of Canada's most famous ballerinas. She was born in Burnaby in 1929. Her dad taught her gymnastics from a young age, but her family couldn't afford dance lessons. When she was ten, her older brother bought her ballet lessons, using income he earned from working at a factory. Her lessons lasted for less than a year, as her brother later lost his job. At fifteen, she began taking lessons again.

Lois was highly talented and decided to make dance her career. Her first professional dance job was with Theatre Under the Stars, performing in summer musicals in Vancouver's Stanley Park. She did this for five years, but it paid next to nothing. The rest of the year, she danced for the Civic Light Opera and musicals in Los Angeles and San Francisco. Lois later joined other companies in Norway and Oklahoma.

Through work, Lois met another dancer who she married in 1949. Together, they worked for the National Ballet of Canada in Toronto. Though this was her dream job, it wasn't easy. Dancers were paid very little when the company wasn't doing well, so money was constantly tight. Many dancers still performed if sick or injured because there were no replacements. Once, Lois performed with a cracked rib. During their first year in Toronto, Lois and her husband lived in a shared house with other dancers. Lois worked long hours, travelled to perform, and even performed outside in bad weather. She held lead roles in *Cinderella*, *Sleeping Beauty*, *Coppélia*, and *Giselle*, and danced for TV shows and sketches.

Eventually, a longstanding knee injury forced Lois to stop dancing, but her involvement in Canadian ballet was far from over. She started the Lois Smith Dance School in Toronto, which later turned into the George Brown College Performing Arts program. She was the chair of the program from 1979–88. She also choreographed dance routines for CBC, the Winnipeg Opera Company, and the Canadian Opera Company. When she retired and moved to Gibsons, BC, in 1988, she started a dance school there.

Lois was awarded the Order of Canada in 1980, and in 1988, the BC Hall of Fame recognized her impressive contributions to culture and entertainment. Lois is remembered for her discipline, serenity, elegance, talent, and love of dance. She left a mark on Canada's dance scene and paved the way for other Canadian ballet dancers.

ACKNOWLEDGEMENTS

I'M GRATEFUL to all those who supported me throughout the writing of *Her Courage Rises*. Thank you to Heritage House Publishing and Lara Kordic for another opportunity to write about trailblazing women and to add women of the Yukon. Thank you to Nandini Thaker for all the support with the publishing process, Monica Miller in marketing and publicity, and to Kimiko Fraser. Thank you to Elysse Bell, whose insight, careful attention to detail, and talented editing made this book infinitely better.

Thank you to Janet Blanchet, Michael Blanchet, Tara Blanchet, Peter Buckland, Arnie Campbell, Patricia Currie, Sara Florence Davidson, Paul Josie, William Josie, Imogene Lim, Jane Montgomery, Vi Mundy, Colm O'Rourke, George Quocksister Jr., Ceridwen Ross Collins, Sheryl Salloum, Dana Simeon, and JJ Verigin.

Thank you to Cathy, Michael and Carmen Kuntz, Alison Martin, my extended family, and the Healey family. To all the readers of my books, many thank-yous and I hope you enjoy this one. Lastly, thank you to Steven Healey for the unwavering commitment, support, and encouragement with this project and with everything.

SELECTED
BIBLIOGRAPHY

* *For a full list of resources, visit www.heritagehouse.ca.*

Ainley, Marianne. *Despite the Odds: Essays on Canadian Women and Science.* 137. Montreal: Vehicle Press, 1990.

Akerman, Joe. "Heal the Land, Heal the People: Strengthening Relationships at Hwaaqw'um in the Salish Sea." Landscape Magazine 6(2), December 15, 2017. https://medium.com/langscape-magazine/heal-the-land-heal-the-people -1tbd62ad3e25. Accessed August 14, 2019.

Albert Johnson, James. "George Carmack: Man of Mystery Who Set Off the Klondike Gold Rush." Kenmore, Washington: Epicenter Press, 2001.

ASTROLab du parc national du Mont-Mégantic. "Helen Sawyer Hogg (1905-1993)." 2022. https://astro-canada.ca/helen_sawyer_hogg-eng. Retrieved November 7, 2021.

Avista Corporation, Spokane Washington. "Crossing Boundaries: The Story of Sophie Morigeau." YouTube video, https://www.youtube.com/watch?v=iu3rQ5n3cLI. Retrieved October 22, 2021.

Backhouse, Frances. *Women of the Klondike.* Vancouver: Whitecap Books, 1995.

Barman, Jean. *Maria Mahoi of the Islands.* Vancouver: New Star Books, 2017.

BC Black History Awareness Society. "Barbara Howard." 2021. https://bcblackhistory .ca/barbara-howard/ Retrieved November 7, 2021.

Beard, Hugh. "Emily Carr: A Woman of All Sorts." Uploaded by Rodney Mercer, December 9, 2016, YouTube video, https://www.youtube.com/watch?v= _asBxfUCu4Q. Accessed January 19, 2019.

Beck, Jason. "Barbara Howard." BC Sports Hall of Fame. https://bcsportshall.com/ honoured_member/barbara-howard/

Blackman, Margaret. *During My Time: Florence Edenshaw Davidson, A Haida Woman.* Vancouver: Douglas and McIntyre, 1982.

Blanchet, M.W. *The Curve of Time.* Vancouver: Gray's Publishing, 1968.

Bramham, Daphne. "Julia Henshaw: A Unique Woman of the War." *Vancouver Sun,* September 8, 2014.

Bridge, Kathryn. *A Passion for the Mountains: The Lives of Don and Phyllis Munday.* Surrey: Rocky Mountain Books, 2006.

Butchart Gardens. "Our Story." 2020. https://www. butchartgardens.com/our-story/. Accessed March 21, 2020.

Canadian War Museum. "Forced Relocation: The Japanese-Canadian Story." 2019. https://www.warmuseum.ca/cwm/exhibitions/chrono/1931forced_e.html Accessed August 12, 2019.

121

Carr, Emily. *Growing Pains: The Autobiography of Emily Carr*. UK: Oxford University Press, 1946.

———. *Sister and I in Alaska*. With an introduction by David Silcox. Vancouver: Figure 1 Publishing, 2014.

CBC *News North*. "Yukon's Black History: Remembering the Intrepid, Courageous Lucille Hunter." https://www.cbc.ca/news/canada/north/lucille-hunter-yukon -hidden-history-1.5907566. Retrieved August 3, 2021.

Chek News. "This Week in History: Alma Russell, Provincial Librarian and Archivist." December 29, 2018.

Clark, Cecil. "Yesterday, Today." *The Victorian* 697, February 23, 1977.

Conn, David. *Raincoast Chronicles 22: Saving Salmon, Sailors and Souls*. 131. Madeira Park: Harbour Publishing, 2013.

Converse, Cathy. *Following the Curve of Time: The Legendary M. Wylie Blanchet*. Victoria: TouchWood Editions, 2008.

Crabb, Michael. "National Ballet Star Lois Smith Dies." *Toronto Star*, January 23, 2011.

Currie, Patricia. "About Dorothy Blackmore." http://www.dorothyblackmore.com. Accessed June 21, 2019.

Doukhobor Discovery Centre. "Doukhobor History." 2022. https://www.doukhobor -museum.org/doukhobor-history. Accessed March 30, 2022.

Duncan, Jennifer. *Frontier Spirit: The Brave Women of the Klondike*. Toronto: Doubleday Canada, 2003.

Essinger, James and Koutzenko, Sandra. *Frankie: How One Woman Prevented a Pharmaceutical Disaster*. North Palm Beach, Florida: Blue Sparrow Books, 2018.

First Nations Drum. "Edith Josie: Here Are the News." December 26, 2000. http://www.first nationsdrum.com/2000/12/edith-josie-here-are-the-news/. Retrieved July 12, 2021.

First Voices. "Nuu-chah-nulth (Barkley) Home Page." http://legacy.firstvoices.com/en /Nuu-chah-nulth/word/2a99bca938427ebc/working Accessed March 8, 2020.

Forbes, Elizabeth. *Wild Roses at Their Feet: Pioneer Women of Vancouver Island*. Vancouver: Evergreen Press Limited, 1971.

Forster, Merna. *100 More Canadian Heroines: Famous and Forgotten Faces*. Toronto: Dundurn Press, 2004.

Gilbert, Catherine Marie. *A Journey Back to Nature: A History of Strathcona Provincial Park*. Victoria: Heritage House, 2021.

Gould, Jan. *Women of British Columbia*. Surrey: Hancock House Publishers, 1975.

Graham, Donald. *Keepers of the Light: A History of British Columbia's Lighthouses and Their Keepers*. Madeira Park: Harbour Publishing, 1985.

Gray, Charlotte. "The True Story of Pauline Johnson: Poet, Provocateur and Champion of Indigenous Rights." *Canadian Geographic*, March 8, 2017.

Great Unsolved Mysteries in Canadian History. "Louis and Sylvia Stark." https://www .canadianmysteries.ca/sites/robinson/murder/castofcharacters/1720en.html. Accessed July 27, 2019.

Green, Valerie and Lynn Gordon-Findlay (illust.). *If More Walls Could Talk: Vancouver Island's Houses from the Past*. Victoria: TouchWood Editions, 2004.

Greenaway, J.E. "Kimiko Murakami: A Picture of Strength." *Salt Spring Today*, December 2005. https://www.yumpu.com/en/document/view/42842171/kimiko -murakami-salt-spring-island-archives. Accessed August 9, 2019.

Haig-Brown, Roderick. *Measure of the Year: Reflections on Home, Family and a Life Fully Lived*. Victoria: TouchWood Editions, 2011.

Haig-Brown, Valerie. *Deep Currents: Roderick and Ann Haig-Brown*. Victoria: Orca Book Publishers, 1997.

Hamilton, Bea. *Salt Spring Island*. Vancouver: Mitchell Press, 1969.

Harbord, Heather. "Capt. Dorothy Blackmore: Pioneer Port Alberni Skipper." *Western Mariner*, June 2004: 21–23.

Holmlund, Mona, and Gail Youngberg. *Inspiring Women: A Celebration of Herstory*. Regina: Coteau Books, 2003.

Horsfield, Margaret. *Cougar Annie's Garden*. Nanaimo: Salal Books, 1999.

Hoy, Jim. "Water Witching." *Symphony in the Flint Hills Field Journal*, 2018. https:// newprairiepress.org/sfh/2018/culture/3. Accessed September 15, 2021.

Hubbard, J. M., David Wildish, and Robert L. Stephenson. *A Century of Marine Science: The St. Andrews Biological Station*. Toronto: University of Toronto Press, 2016.

Hume, Stephen. "Canada 150: Salty, Fearless "Ma" Murray edited Lillooet Newspaper." *Vancouver Sun*, February 2, 2017.

Humphreys, Danda. *On the Street Where You Live: Sailors, Solicitors and Stargazers of Early Victoria*. Surrey: Heritage House, 2001.

Kahn, Charles. *Salt Spring: The Story of an Island*. Madeira Park: Harbour Publishing, 1998.

Kilian, Crawford. "On the Trail of the Yukon's Black Pioneers." *The Tyee*, November 18, 2009. https://thetyee.ca/Life/2009/11/18/BlackPioneers/. Retrieved August 3, 2021.

Layland, Michael. "Our History: When Capt. Cook First Found the Island." *Times Colonist*, October 3, 2014. https://www.timescolonist.com/our-history-when-capt -cook-first-found-the-island-1.1413933. Accessed September 1, 2019.

"Lilian Bland: Ireland's First Female Aviator." http://www.lilianbland.ie. Accessed August 14, 2019.

Louis, Adam. "Louis: Hold up, who was this Ma Murray?" *Vancouver Island Free Daily*, April 20, 2021. https://www.vancouverislandfreedaily.com/opinion/louis-hold-up -who-was-this-ma-murray/. Retrieved July 12, 2021.

Maffi, Luisa. "Learning Our Language is Like Learning to See in Full Color: An Interview with Gisèle Maria Martin (Tla-o-qui-aht)." *Landscape Magazine*, November 6, 2019. https://medium.com/langscape-magazine/learning-ourlanguage-is-like -learning-to-see-in-full-color-an-interview-with-gisele-mariamartin-fd497ebf86a1.

Mason, Adrienne. *West Coast Adventures: Shipwrecks, Lighthouses, and Rescues Along Canada's West Coast*. 135. Canmore: Altitude Publishing Canada, 2003.

Merriman, Alec. "Vagabond Cruising in Coastal Waters." *Daily Colonist*, July 7, 1968.

Museum at Campbell River. "Elizabeth Quocksister Collection." https://campbellriver .crmuseum.ca/category/gallery/elizabeth-quocksister-collection. Accessed October 22, 2019.

Museum at Campbell River. "Haig-Brown Heritage House." 2014. http://www.haig
-brown.bc.ca. Accessed June 23, 2019.

National Film Board of Canada. "Haida Carver." 1964.

Neering, Rosemary. *Wild West Women: Travellers, Adventurers and Rebels*. Vancouver:
Whitecap Books, 2000.

Norquist, Suzanne. "Delina Noel: Mine Prospector and Trapper." Heroes, Heroines,
and History, April 10, 2020. https://www.hhhistory.com/2020/04/delina-noel
-mine-prospector-and-trapper.html. Retrieved January 1, 2022.

North Island Gazette. "The Adventurous Life of Lilian Bland." May 11, 2016.

Pacific Motor Boat. "It's Miss Captain to You, Mate!" December 1945: 46–47.

Parks Canada. "Barbara Touchie (1931–2014)." https://www.canada.ca/en/parks
-canada/news/2016/09/barbara-touchie-1931-2014.html. Accessed March 8, 2020.

Parks Canada. "Hawaiian Settlement on Russell Island." https://www.pc.gc.ca/en
/pn-np/bc/gulf/culture/hawaienne-hawaiian. Accessed March 7, 2020.

Peterson, Jan. *The Albernis, 1860–1922*. Victoria: Oolichan Books, 1992.

Price, John and Ningping Yu. *A Woman in Between: Searching for Dr. Victoria Chung*.
Vancouver: Chinese Canadian Historical Society of British Columbia, 2019.

Redford, Gabrielle. "Why Should We Care About Marine Worms?" National Wildlife
Federation, April 1, 2001. https://www.nwf.org/en/Magazines/National
Wildlife/2001/Marine-Worms. Accessed June 23, 2019.

Roberts, Eric. *Salt Spring Saga: An Exciting Story of Pioneer Days*. Salt Spring Island:
Driftwood, 1962.

Robertson, Leslie. *Standing Up with Ga'axsta'las: Jane Constance Cook and the Politics of
Memory, Church and Custom*. Vancouver: UBC Press, 2012.

Royal BC Museum. "Alma Russell." 2014. http://transcribe.royalbcmuseum.bc.ca/
alma-russell. Accessed March 31, 2022.

Royal BC Museum. "Hannah Maynard." https://royalbcmuseum.bc.ca/exhibits/bc
-archives-time machine/galler10/frames/maynard.htm. Accessed July 23, 2019.

Salloum, Sheryl. *The Life of Bohemian, Rancher and Artist Sonia Cornwall, 1919-2006*.
Halfmoon Bay: Caitlin Press Inc., 2015.

Salt Spring Island Historical Society. "Amazing Women of Salt Spring Island." 2008.
http://saltspringarchives.com/women.pdf. Accessed August 14, 2019.

Sidney, Angela. *Tagish Tlaagú*. Whitehorse: Council for Yukon Indians and the
Government of Yukon, 1982.

Smith, Shirleen and Vuntut Gwitchin First Nation. *People of the Lakes: Stories of Our
Van Tat Gwich'in Elders/Googwandak Nakhuach'ànjòo Van Tat Gwitch'in*. Edmonton:
University of Alberta Press, 2009.

Smithsonian Postal Museum. "Belinda Mulrooney: The Richest Woman in the
Klondike." https://postalmuseum.si.edu/exhibition/as-precious-as-gold-stories
-from-the-gold-rush-extraordinary-women/belinda-mulrooney-the. Retrieved
January 1, 2022.

Stark-Wallace, Marie. "From Slavery to Freedom: The History of the Stark Family."
Gulf Islands Driftwood, ten-part series, 1979.

Tarasoff, Koozma. "Anna Markova: A Doukhobor Martyr." November 7, 2011. http://spirit-wrestlers.blogspot.com. Accessed March 30, 2022.

Taylor, Robert Ratcliffe. *The Spencer Mansion: A House, a Home, and an Art Gallery.* Victoria: TouchWood Editions, 2021.

Terry, Pat. "Capt. Dorothy Blackmore of Port Alberni, Follows Dad." *Vancouver Sun,* December 6, 1937.

Toronto Star Weekly. "Women Invade Traditional Male Domains." July 14, 1946.

Unwin, Peter. *Canadian Folk: Portraits of Remarkable Lives.* Toronto: Dundurn Press, 2013.

US National Park Service. "Shaaw Tláa (Kate Carmack)." 2021. https://www.nps.gov /people/kate-carmack.htm. Retrieved August 11, 2021

USCC Doukhobors. "Kootenay USCC Ladies Organization: History and Philosophy." 2013. http://www.usccdoukhobors.org/usccladies/usccladies.htm. Accessed March 31, 2022.

Victoria Heritage Foundation. "1040 Moss Street." 2021. https://victoriaheritage foundation.ca/HReg/Rockland/Moss1040.html. Accessed October 14, 2021.

Vuntut Gwitchin First Nation. "A Short Autobiography by Edith Josie." https://www .oldcrow.ca/edith.htm. Retrieved July 12, 2021.

Weder, Adele. "Artist Hazel Wilson Stitched Haida History into Blankets." *The Globe and Mail,* May 31, 2016. https://www.theglobeandmail.com/news/national/artist -hazel-wilson-stitched-haida-history-into-blankets/article30224588/. Retrieved July 20, 2021.

West Coast Advocate. "Police Boat Makes Thrilling Rescue on Stormy West Coast." March 14, 1946.

Whysall, Steve. "Revisiting Cougar Annie's Garden." *Vancouver Sun,* February 25, 2016.

Wilks, Claire Weissman. *The Magic Box: The Eccentric Genius of Hannah Maynard.* Toronto: Exile Editions Limited, 1980.

Wilson, Bob. "Ruth Masters: Lifetime of Stand Up for Parks, Wilderness and Wildlife." Federation of Mountain Clubs of British Columbia.

Wolf, Jim. "Isaburo Kishida: British Columbia Pioneer Japanese Landscape Designer." *Sitelines: British Columbia Society of Landscape Architects,* February 2003. http:// www.urbanecology.ca/documents/Journal%20 Articles/Sitelines2003.pdf. Accessed March 23, 2020.

Women's Museum of Ireland. "Lilian Bland: Pioneering Aviatrix." https://womens museumofireland.ie/articles/lilian-bland. Accessed August 14, 2019.

Wong, May Q. *City in Colour: Rediscovered Stories of Victoria's Multicultural Past.* Victoria: TouchWood Editions, 2018.

Wynard, Flo. *Martha Black: Her Story from the Gold Fields of Dawson to the Halls of Parliament.* Whitehorse: Caribou Classic, 2007.

Yee, Paul. *Chinatown: An Illustrated History of the Chinese Communities of Victoria, Vancouver, Calgary, Edmonton, Winnipeg, Toronto, Montreal and Halifax.* Toronto: James Lorimer and Company, 2005.

Yukon Archives. "Hidden History: Black History of the Yukon. Lucille Hunter." 2007. http://tc.gov.yk.ca/archives/hiddenhistory/en/women.html. Retrieved August 3, 2021.

IMAGE CREDITS

The illustrator's renderings of the women in this book are based on the following photographic sources.

Edith Berkeley, page 82. University Archives and Special Collections, University Library, University of Saskatchewan.

Martha Black, page 112. From the House of Commons' collection.

Dorothy Blackmore, page 56. From Patricia and Bob Currie.

Capi Blanchet, page 20. From Michael Blanchet.

Lilian Bland, page 54. From http://www.lilianbland.ie.

Rosemary Brown, page 114. Illustration from Royal BC Museum image I-32427.

Jennie Butchart, page 38. Illustration based on City of Victoria Archives image M00552.

Kate Carmack/Shaaw Tláa, page 58. Yukon Archives, James Albert Johnson fonds, 82/341, #22.

Emily Carr, page 36. Illustration from City of Vancouver Archives Image, CVA 136-034.

Nellie Cashman, page 52. Illustration from Royal BC Museum image D-01775.

Victoria Chung, page 76. United Church of Canada Pacific Mountain Regional Council Archives, Oriental Home and School fonds, P-31/1, image 33.

Ga'axsta'las/Jane Constance Cook, page 108. Illustration from Royal BC Museum image H-07220.

Sonia Cornwall, page 34. Courtesy of the Sonia Cornwall Family Collection.

Florence Edenshaw Davidson, page 30. Photo by Ulli Steltzer, Courtesy of Princeton University Library with permission from family.

Alice Freeman (Faith Fenton), page 14. Photo: Faith Fenton. Source: Library and Archives Canada/a212241k.

Mary Ann Gyves/Tuwa'hwiye Tusium Gosselim, page 94. Illustration based on original image held at the Salt Spring Archives.

Ann Elmore Haig-Brown, page 102. Museum at Campbell River.

Julia Henshaw, page 80. Illustration from City of Vancouver Archives Image, Port P1073.

Helen Sawyer Hogg, page 74. Courtesy of Toronto Public Library, TSPA_0055292F.

Barbara Howard, page 116. Illustration from City of Vancouver Archives Image, CVA 371-1643.

Lucille Hunter, page 46. Yukon Archives, Richard Harrington fonds, 79/27, #277.

E. Pauline Johnson/Tekahionwake, page 10. Illustration from City of Vancouver Archives Image, Port P637.

Edith Josie, page 8. From the *Whitehorse Star*.

Frances Oldham Kelsey, page 72. Reference image from the Library of Congress, Prints & Photographs Division, U.S. News & World Report Magazine Collection, USNWR-8269.

Maria Mahoi, page 92. Illustration based on original image held at the Salt Spring Archives (Accession number: 2008009009).

Anna Petrovna Markova, page 88. From JJ Verigin and the Union of Spiritual Communities of Christ.

Ruth Masters, page 68. Photo by Ed Brooks.

Hannah Maynard, page 24. Illustration from Royal BC Museum image F-05043.

Sophie Morigeau, page 44. Original photo courtesy of Derek Lapierre and the Morigeau Family Tree Project.

Belinda Mulrooney, page 40. From the Yakima Valley Museum.

Phyllis Munday, page 70. Illustration from Royal BC Museum image I-68123.

Kimiko Murakami, page 86. Illustration based on original image held at the Salt Spring Archives (Accession number: 2004005002).

Margaret "Ma" Murray, page 12. Fort St. John North Peace Museum, 1988.05.181 photo.

Delina Noel, page 48. Based on an original photo from the Bralorne Pioneer Museum.

Minnie Paterson, page 62. Alberni Valley Museum Photo PN11869.

Evelyn Penrose, page 110. From *ABC Bookworld.*

Elizabeth Quocksister, page 22. Museum at Campbell River.

Cougar Annie/Ada Annie Rae Author, page 42. Illustration from Royal BC Museum image C-04904.

Kathleen Rockwell, page 28. University of Washington Special Collections, JWS13134.

Isabella Mainville Ross, page 90. Illustration from Royal BC Museum image F-01280.

Alma Russell, page 104. Illustration from Royal BC Museum image H-03167.

Catherine Schubert, page 66. Illustration from Royal BC Museum image A-03081.

Angela Sidney/Ch'óonehte' Ma Stóow, page 18. Yukon Archives, Janice Hamilton fonds, 2008/130, #15. and Yukon Archives, Janice Hamilton fonds, 2008/130, #1.

Lois Smith, page 118. Original Image Courtesy of the National Ballet of Canada.

Sara Ellen Spencer, page 106. Illustration from Royal BC Museum image B-06991.

Emma Stark, page 84. Illustration based on original image held at the Salt Spring Archives (Accession number: 989024010).

Barbara Touchie/Sičquuʔuƛ, page 98. Photo by Melody Charlie, Courtesy of Vi Mundy and Family.

Émilie Tremblay, page 50. Société historique du Saguenay, FPH65, P05587.

Hazel Anna Wilson/Jut-Ke-Nay, page 26. From Dana Simeon.

Nellie Yip Quong, page 96. Original Image Courtesy of Imogene Lim and Starlet Lum and Vancouver Heritage Foundation, The Places That Matter Community History Resource.

HALEY HEALEY is a high school counsellor and the bestselling author of *On Their Own Terms: True Stories of Trailblazing Women of Vancouver Island* and *Flourishing and Free: More Stories of Trailblazing Women of Vancouver Island*. She lives in Nanaimo and enjoys exploring Vancouver Island's trails, waters, and wilderness.

KIMIKO FRASER is an illustrator and historian-in-training. She grew up constantly making—drawing, painting, knitting, sculpting, bookbinding, etc.—and has never learned how to stop. She holds a Bachelor of Arts (honours History, major Visual Arts) from the University of Victoria. She works with many mediums to create her illustrations, including watercolour, digital, ink, and tea. Most of her work is inspired by her interest in plants, history, and folktales.